# HOUSE ARREST

## Rick Gannon

First published in 2017 in the UK

3P Publishing

C E C, London Road

Corby

NN17 5EU

A catalogue number for this book is available from the British Library

ISBN 978-1-911559-34-4

Cover Design: Jamie Rae

To my beautiful wife and soul mate,
Lorraine and amazing children,
Ben and Charlotte.
You guys are my rock!

# CONTACT DETAILS

If you would like to contact me to discuss anything (property related) then please feel free to drop me a line or tag me in a post:-

www.newerapropertysolutions.co.uk (main website)

The HMO Community Group (our Facebook HMO page)

Rick Gannon UK (my public Facebook page)

Rick@newerapropertysolutions.co.uk (my email)

# Contents

# Acknowledgements

In writing this book I have many people to thank. These people have been an inspiration to me, not only in property, but in business and life.

I would like to thank my wife, Lorraine, for her unconditional support in everything that I do. You are my rock.

My amazing son, Ben, for just being Ben; for being so inspirational and loving. I would also like to thank my beautiful daughter, Charlotte, for being such an amazing and wonderful person, and supportive sister to Ben.

I would like to thank my family for putting up with me for so long (there's more to come), and for believing in our business.

I would like to thank everyone that has been a part of our training programme and to those that have taken action and changed their lives for the better. You are all inspirational.

To all of those that have helped in the writing of this book over the past eighteen months, it has taken to research, write, and publish this book. With that in mind, thank you to Andy and Caroline at 3P Publishing for helping to make this happen.

And finally, thank you to you for buying this book, and taking the time to read it.

# Introduction

Can I ask you a quick question? Did you buy this book to learn how to get rich quick and become a millionaire in a month from a totally passive property portfolio?

If you did, then don't read any more! Put this book down now and go and waste your hard-earned cash on something else. I want you to understand, before you invest your time reading this book, that Houses in Multiple Occupation are far from passive and they will not make you a millionaire in a month!

If you bought this book because you want to make a positive change in your life and start a successful property business that you can live off forever. If you are prepared to work harder in the first year than you have ever worked before and you are prepared to grind your fingers to the bone. If you are fed up of all the stories that you hear and read about from people making gazillions of pounds each week from HMOs while sitting on a beach in the Caribbean and if you are looking for no frills and factual information on how it really is, then this is the book for you. Read on my friend.

# Chapter 1
# Sucker Punch

"**I** 'm so sorry to have to break this news to you over the phone. If there is anything else I can do, then please get in touch."

I put the phone down feeling remorseful. I zipped up my fleece and continued to place items into an evidence bag. An old watch with a faded brown leather strap, a black leather wallet with not much inside except for a few old supermarket receipts, and a few loose coins, no more than £3.00 in mixed denominations. I noted the items in my pocketbook. My hands were shaking; it was cold, very cold, and it didn't help that I was writing by torchlight as the power had gone. The electric metre had run out.

It was early on a wet, cold February morning and I was standing in someone's living room. I was an operational response Taser-armed police officer for West Mercia Police. The job was a sudden death; reports from a neighbour that she hadn't seen her friend for a few days and there was a strange smell coming from the house.

Upon arriving, I knocked on the door. No response. I shouted "Hello, it's the police!" and again no response. I took out my police issue torch and shone it through the window, but the curtains were drawn.

This only meant one thing. Based on the information from the neighbour, I would have to force entry. It wasn't difficult. I quickly realised the door wasn't locked – as I ran towards it about to force entry but it opened. I went flying through and nearly landed on the couch.

The smell hit me immediately. As a police officer, you know that smell. Imagine the worst smell you have ever experienced and multiply it by 100 and that wouldn't even come close to the smell of a decomposing body. I quickly regained my balance and tried to familiarise myself with my surroundings. It was dark and there was no power. I went to open the curtain to allow the light from the outside street lamp to assist me, but I quickly realised that what I thought was a curtain in the window when I stood outside was, in fact, a sea of flies. They were everywhere; thousands of them.

I quickly had to go back outside to get some air. From experience, I knew what I was about to embark upon. I recomposed myself and went inside scanning the room with my torch. There he was, in his dressing gown and sitting on the couch next to the electric fire which was now switched off due to the lack of power.

By the discomposure, it was clear he was dead. That was obvious, coupled with the stench. Poor chap. It was impossible to tell how long, but I would guess at least two weeks.

As if it wasn't bad enough having to look at this poor chap, my job had only just begun. As I now had to undress him and search his corpse for anything that may indicate foul play. I had dealt with many dead bodies in my career (into the hundreds) and as you roll a corpse over, any air left in the lungs or any fluids will escape. Not good!

Fortunately, the coroner arrived quickly and my job was over. I managed to finish my shift on time, but I was desperate for a shower. All I could smell was death.

I arrived home on time at around 07:30, feeling a little despondent and tired. I walked into the kitchen and greeted my wife, Lorraine, and then went upstairs to kiss my children. A ritual I always followed after a night shift. I went to see my beautiful daughter Charlotte who was then aged five. I kissed her; she was her usual happy self and getting ready for school. I then walked over the landing into the front bedroom to my son Ben's room, who was aged nine. I could see that Ben looked troubled.

"Hey Ben, are you ok?" I asked. He replied, "No, not really Dad. I'm worried about something." "Ok, what is it? Maybe I can help." Ben then said something to me that would be the catalyst for me making a total change and re-evaluating my life. "Dad," Ben said, "Why can't I play football like my friends?" Wow, this was a total sucker punch, and I didn't know how to reply. You see, Ben has quadriplegic cerebral palsy. He was born almost three months premature. He has no use of his legs at all and only limited use of his arms. He is totally wheelchair-bound and dependent on around the clock care from us. I didn't honestly know how I could answer this; I'm his dad, I have to make this right. "It's ok Ben, we will find a way," I said with a lump in my throat, not knowing how the hell I could make this better for him.

We had a cuddle, and as tears welled up in my eyes, I reassured him that everything would be ok. I went to my room not knowing how I could help, but knowing for sure that I had to make some serious life changes. I had a shower and went straight to bed. My head was confused and very full!

I slept badly and eventually got up at around midday. I could never sleep past midday on a night shift; it plays havoc with your body clock. I washed and dressed and went downstairs to to see my wife Lorraine, who at the time worked from home as a Procurement Consultant. We had a discussion about life in general, and I told her about my shift and how depressing it was. We then spoke about Ben and how we could help him with his disability and how he could achieve his goal of playing football.

I knew that we had some changes to make. I knew that as Ben grew older he would be more demanding and that would mean both of us having to devote more time to him. I needed to leave my job as a police officer.

Lorraine and I discussed this and both agreed it would be the only thing to do to help Ben's progress, but what could I do? We had a modest mortgage, credit card bills, a car loan, two hungry children to feed, and a huge hungry dog!

Lorraine suggested that we attend a local group in Worcester that met once a month to talk about property. She had met someone at a networking meeting, and he had given her the name of the group. Not being from a corporate background, I couldn't think of anything worse at that time in my life than meeting strangers and "NETWORKING", but I was dragged along anyway. Sound familiar?

As we entered the room, you couldn't miss the big banners with bold statements. I remember thinking 'Oh this is ridiculous! No way is that achievable. It's absolute rubbish and, in fact, it's probably all illegal!'

There must have been around thirty to forty others in the room, all of whom were total strangers to me. Lorraine was off doing her networking thing leaving me to fend for myself in a room full of strangers! I didn't do idle chat with strangers.

Thankfully we were quickly ushered to our seats by a very friendly host who introduced himself and welcomed all the new "first-timers."

"Ladies and gentleman I'm pleased to introduce our first speaker of the night..."

I think I was in a trance at this point, not only had I just been "networking" for the first time in my entire life, I now had to sit and listen to someone that I had nothing in common with, and little interest in, whatsoever blabbering on about a load of crap. I was sure to hate it!

As I sat there, in all honesty, I was texting someone from work and mocking my current situation. As he began to speak, I put my phone down and listened. The chap on the stage was a motivational business coach, something that I had no experience of before, but I was gripped straight away; he was talking about me. Everything he was saying was about me! How did he know so much about me: we had never met? He, of course, wasn't really talking about me but it certainly felt like it. I could resonate with almost every word, every sentence. It was a profound moment, and it gave me a complete paradigm shift.

I was used to dealing with rufty tufty police officers and all the bad things in life. It was my job to pick up the pieces (sometimes literally) when things went wrong in other people's lives. But for now, at this moment, I was somewhere else, listening intensively to this motivational speaker, all the thoughts in my head had gone, and I was just focusing on his voice. His words at that moment made me realise that I could achieve much more than I ever thought I was capable of.

Once the presentation finished, it was time for "NETWORKING" again! Urghh, boring conversation about stuff; I didn't understand the very thought of talking to strangers about stuff. Their stuff was bound to be better than my stuff. I didn't relish the thought of any of it; then the chap that was just on the stage came over and said hello. He asked what I did for a living and when I told him he immediately turned to another person in the room and said, "Oh, she's a police officer too!"

What are the chances? Another police officer that was also looking to change their life for the better. And what's more, she had only retired a few weeks ago from the same station as me! What are the chances?

We got to chatting and we quickly went on to the subject of HMOs (Houses in Multiple Occupation) and how she was using this as her main strategy. She was also very close to replacing her previous income as a police officer. I was engrossed. Surely this had to be real? I trusted her. She was a cop just like me and I trusted cops. Cops were my family.

I was, however, a little confused, as my only experience of HMOs was obtaining warrants from the court and raiding them to arrest drug dealers and prostitutes! Why on earth would I want to own one? We chatted and the more I listened, the more interested I became; I was now feeling inquisitive.

It was a strange feeling. In the police, we are taught to 'Assume nothing. Believe nobody and check everything'. It's called the ABC of policing. I lived by that mantra for over thirteen years. I suppose I still do to a degree, but here I was, only two hours later thinking, 'I can do this'.

Lorraine and I had a quick chat, and we decided that investing in HMOs was something that we wanted to pursue. First, we had to educate ourselves and neither of us had the first clue on how to run an HMO. Due to my experiences, did I really want to?

# Chapter 2
# Early Days

I joined the police quite late in life aged thirty-one. I suppose I was pursuing a childhood dream. My dad always wanted to join but was never successful, so I guess some of it was for him. Owing to a really sad set of circumstances, he never did get to see me join.

My mum and dad divorced a few years before I enrolled and, stupidly, I took sides and decided to estrange myself from my dad. I didn't speak to him for three years. I decided in December 2001 I would contact him and make amends for being such an idiot. But unfortunately, I didn't get the chance as early January 2002 my dad took a fall in his flat and cut his head badly on a glass on the floor. He went to bed and passed away in his sleep after bleeding to death, aged fifty-four. I never got the chance to make things better, something I will carry for the rest of my life.

Before joining the police, I had a few jobs. I suppose I was a bit lost. I left school at sixteen and joined the Army. I didn't last long and it wasn't my thing, so I left after serving only a few months and subsequently went to college and became qualified as a chef and then a chef assessor. I worked in some local hotels and pubs in and around Cheshire and my hometown of Warrington before being promoted to relief manager for the company I was with the time. This involved moving every couple of weeks to different locations around the country and living out of a suitcase, which was great as I had no ties. I was single and I was heading up the career ladder in catering.

During September 1992, I was working in Worcester as a relief manager for a gastro-type pub. I had been there for about three weeks and was getting quite friendly with one of the part-time waitresses, and I eventually plucked up enough courage to ask her out on a date, which, to my surprise, she said yes! Lorraine and I got married eight years later. We have been together for an amazing twenty-four years, and Lorraine continues to be my best friend, business partner, and soul mate!

After being together for a while, Lorraine and I decided that we could both do better than working for a large company where most of the senior management team didn't even know our names. We began looking elsewhere. We both wanted to buy our own pub, but we had no money at all. I eventually left the pub trade, and I took what I thought was going to be a temporary position with a finance company as a development manager while Lorraine pursued a career as a chartered accountant. We did this for a few years, and my job led to a promotion to a position of area manager, which came with a move to Nottingham. We bought a new-build house from plan; we stayed there for a couple of years, but we still had this burning ambition to own our own business and continued to look for a pub to run.

After only a couple of months of intense searching, we found the ideal place for us, not to far away from Hereford. It was on the market advertised for lease for ten years, and the asking price was £15,000, but we had no money.

We had no property training whatsoever at this point, and we didn't have the first clue as to how to structure a deal, so we asked Lorraine's parents if there was any chance they would be able to help us. They said yes, and they loaned us the £15K we needed to buy the pub lease.

I resigned from my job with the finance company and we bought the lease on the pub, which involved moving back from Nottingham to Hereford. We decided to rent our house in Nottingham in case anything went wrong so we would still have a place to live. We then became accidental landlords. After purchasing the lease on the pub, Lorraine and I traded it for a few years, ourselves, and built the business up from the ground. About two years into the agreement, the owner approached us and asked if we would like to buy the freehold. We had managed to rustle up enough money for the deposit, and we purchased the property for £175,000. The property was a vast building over four floors with two flats and five en-suite letting bedrooms, two bars, a snug, and a catering kitchen. It also had a very large barn outside. Over the years, it had many uses: a skittle alley, a shooting range, a small function room, a local carpenter's workshop, and the local village post office that Lorraine's mum ran!

We decided that the barns were too big for us to manage and look after. They didn't bring in much revenue, so we advertised them on the market, although we had no idea really what they were worth.

Within about a week, we had a viewing and an offer of £90,000. The purchaser called us and asked for a meeting as he wanted to discuss his purchase strategy. We didn't have a clue what he meant, but we agreed.

During the meeting over coffee, the potential buyer explained that he would like to give us a £2,000 deposit that would be non-refundable if we gave him an exclusive lockout agreement. This would prevent us selling it to anyone else while he sought planning permission to turn it into a dwelling, which may take up to six months. We had nothing to lose, so we agreed. He paid his £2,000, and we signed the documents and waited. It didn't take six months; it only took about eight weeks. He was successful in obtaining the permission in turning the barn into a residential four-bedroom property.

We completed the sale and, all of a sudden, we had created about £90,000 from an asset that we rarely used. We agreed that the money from this sale would go directly to Lorraine's parents to pay them back the initial leasehold money and the rest as a thank you for helping us out in the first place. After all, we wouldn't have been able to do this on our own: win-win! This got us thinking. We had traded the pub now for over three years. It was ticking along and we had created a decent business. My childhood ambition to join the police was still burning inside me and I wasn't getting any younger. Lorraine and I decided to move forward and to lease our pub to tenants which meant that we still owned the asset and we could make a bit of rent on top.

We advertised the lease in a national pub sales magazine. The asking price was £50, 000 for the goodwill of the business. This was a one-off fee that was, of course, non-refundable, and we charged at that time £28,000 a year in rent. To our surprise, within about four weeks we had an offer of the full asking price. It was one of the local customers that had a fair bit of pub experience, and four weeks later we had completed the deal.

To break this down, we initially purchased the lease for £15,000. We then purchased the freehold for £175,000; we sold the barns for £90,000, and we then created and sold a lease for £50,000.

We created £140,000 from this business. In effect, it only cost us £35,000 to buy it, but don't forget we also charged £28,000 a year to the tenants. The amazing thing is that we still owned this property and it remained under lease after all these years still achieving great rental. We were offered over half a million a few years back to purchase the property by a national pub company, but we declined.

We decided to sell our house in Nottingham and, with the money, we raised a deposit to buy a run-down cottage for £80,000 back in a lovely village in Worcester where Lorraine grew up and her family still lived.

We spent a lot of time refurbishing the cottage to make it a nice home for years to come, a home that saw the birth of our beautiful children.

# Chapter 3
# Making a Change


My joining date for West Midlands Police was February 2002. I was thirty-one when I enrolled, which isn't unheard of in the police as many join late after leaving service in the Armed Forces; nevertheless, it was quite an eye-opener.

Lorraine and I had been married for several years and had been trying for a family for a while. I was working long twelve to fourteen hour shifts and Lorraine was working 9 to 5 in her accountancy role, so we rarely got to see each other. I remember waking up after a night shift, which back then was nine hours, seven nights in every four weeks. It was a killer, no pun intended. I walked into the kitchen of our cottage and Lorraine was standing there.  She just came out with it and told me we were going to have a baby! I don't mind admitting that I cried as it was just amazing news and long awaited. Nothing now mattered at that point and I was the proudest man in the world! Wow. I now had responsibilities, and I had to step up! I had to be careful at work, and I had to look after myself.  I was going to be a dad!

I was riot trained in the police. We call it Public Order trained. I was busy with my team one Sunday at a Birmingham City football match when I got a call from Lorraine. She was very calm and told me she had to go into hospital as she was bleeding badly. She still had ten weeks left of her pregnancy, so surely the baby wasn't ready to meet us yet. I spoke to my supervisor and was released from duty. A colleague escorted me back to my station in Bourneville Lane, Birmingham. I didn't even change from my riot gear; I just got into my car and drove to Worcester Royal Hospital where I met Lorraine in the maternity ward. Her parents, sister, and her sister's boyfriend were there already.

Twenty-four hours later, our son Ben was born by emergency C-section. He was tiny and weighed 3lb 15 ounces. He was really small and looked so vulnerable he was almost three months premature! He was taken straight to intensive care in the high dependency NICU unit where he stayed for four weeks, which seemed like an eternity!

Amazingly, Ben did exceptionally well and after four weeks, he was allowed home. Things were great! In fact, they couldn't have been better.

Ben had been home for about six months. He cried a lot but babies do that, right? In fact, he cried pretty much from the moment he woke to the moment he went back to sleep.

One morning Lorraine left the house early to take Ben for a routine checkup. I was up and mentally preparing myself for work when about two hours later Lorraine pulled onto the driveway and got Ben out of the car. She walked into the house and burst out crying. I had no idea what was wrong. I comforted her and, eventually, Lorraine managed to tell me that our doctor had told her that Ben had a condition called Cerebral Palsy. In layman's terms, this meant that his brain was starved of oxygen during the birthing process and it caused an infection resulting in brain damage. The doctor told Lorraine that Ben would never walk or lead a normal life, we just didn't know what to do. This turned our whole world upside down. I began to see things in slow motion. I will never forget that day, ever.

I didn't go into work. Lorraine, Ben, and I did a lot of cuddling. It was emotional; we discussed the future and what it would be like. Truth be known, we didn't have a clue what to do. There is no cure for Cerebral Palsy. We were powerless.

As the months passed, we tried to carry on as normal hoping that the doctor had got things wrong, consistently living in hope. Lorraine and I had decided that after hearing this news, we needed to dedicate all our time to Ben to help him grow and flourish. I took a career break from the Police. I guess we panicked and we decided to go and buy another pub as that's all we knew. Thinking we could have a decent income and we would employ staff to manage the business allowing us to spend time with Ben.

We were a couple of years in. The pub was doing well, and we were spending time together. As a family, we decided now that we wanted to grow the business, and over the following two years, we had accrued a chain of gastropubs with a total of five establishments dotted around Worcester. Some we leased and others we owned, but the more we grew, it was apparent that this was taking us away from our initial goals. We weren't making a huge amount of money. In fact, I guess we were just breaking even as the good pubs paid for the bad ones. It was then that the Government decided to put the levy up on alcohol, and then the smoking ban came. This took about £3,000 a week from our weekly profit overnight!

Lorraine and I discussed this over the coming weeks and we reflected on our decision in running a pub company. What was our reason why? It was to spend time with Ben and help him grow and flourish. Suddenly, the penny dropped! We were so wrapped up in our business that we were spending less time with Ben than we were before, so we decided to revert to how things had been previously. We sold some of the pubs, and the others that were on lease we handed back to the owners. We kept one; the first one that we bought as we were too emotionally attached to sell it.

The great thing about being in the police is they do allow, under certain circumstances, for you to take a career break and allow you to return within a five-year period, which is exactly what I did.

Not long after I had re-joined, Lorraine and I were expecting our second child. We were both full of excitement and, of course, lots of anxiety as it was always in the back of our mind that things may go wrong. If it did, how would we cope?

Eight months later, our little bundle of joy was born and we had a beautiful, healthy little girl called Charlotte. Although she was slightly premature, there were no complications which, as you can imagine, was a huge relief for us.

We were back in the swing of things and the years ran away with us. The kids were growing up fast. Ben, as the doctors predicted, was completely wheelchair-bound, but we tried to lead as normal a life as we could and tried hard not to let his disability rule us. Before I knew it, I was a qualified Police Sergeant and in a Temporary Sergeant's Role. I was heading up the career ladder, and I was a respected leader. I did, at times, enjoy my job, but I was always aware that it wasn't taking me towards my goal and the penny didn't drop until that morning that Ben and I had our five-minute conversation.

After talking to my police colleague at our first property meeting, Lorraine and I decided to enroll into a property course. We were quite sure that we wanted to pursue property. We had tried other things, and they just didn't work; all we wanted was extra time to spend with our family and this might give us that opportunity. We both enrolled in a one-day property training day in Birmingham. We felt very pleased and enthusiastic that this may just be what we were looking for.

Life carried on as normal for a while. Ben was growing fast and he was starting to notice that he was different from his friends. He was subtle about it, but you could see him watching the other kids as they played. Ben doesn't often talk about his feelings and emotions, but I could tell that certain things were beginning to bother him. How on earth could I help him to play football? He can't walk for heaven's sake!

Lorraine and I headed towards the crowded room. There must have been over a hundred people there, all keen and looking at how they could invest in property. All wanting to change their life for the greater good.

As we walked in, we were met by some very happy faces, shaking our hands with vigour as we entered. We shuffled our way to the closest seats and sat eagerly waiting to learn.

A group of about five people gathered on the stage and the audience began to quiet down. A friendly male with a heavy Birmingham accent began to speak, a likeable chap who welcomed us to the room and began telling us about his property journey and how it had changed his life. We then had a similar speech from a lady and then we were introduced to the main speaker for the day, who walked cheerfully onto the stage to rapturous amounts of applause. The room went silent as he began to tell his story. He was well-educated, had graduated from business school, and he went on to run his own business. He told us how, against all the odds, it had failed, and he was forced to close it, but from investing in property he had managed to become financially free in a relatively short period of time.

I found his story fascinating. He remains a great friend to this day. Lorraine and I decided that we needed to educate ourselves further and decided to join, and pay, for the next level of education, which was a three-day event in Birmingham. We were excited and very nervous as we were about to embark on a very different journey that would take us well out of our comfort zone. Things were about to change! Little did we know how much.

# Chapter 4
# Why Choose HMOs?

I was on an early shift, 7am to 3pm, and I had already typed out my request. I was really nervous as I didn't know what to expect. I walked into my supervisor's office and closed the door. I was, by now, no longer a Temporary Sergeant, even though I had been in the role for around three years. Although I was very competent at my job, I didn't say the correct things in my interview and was scored down, so I was subsequently demoted back to PC. This is the norm in the police, and it's a bit of a ping-pong game to get promoted. As long as you say the correct thing in the interview, you will get through. So all the politically-correct bods with next to no experience on the front-line usually get promoted, leaving us seasoned, well-experienced, not so PC folk behind. The interview process is extremely archaic and needs a shakeup.

I handed over my letter to my supervisor and explained that I had decided to request a career break. As Ben was becoming more dependent as he was getting older, he was our main priority. I needed to spend time with him on his transition year to high school. My supervisor was surprised, but supportive, and said she would forward this to our inspector.

When you take a career break in the Police Service, it means that you are still a police officer, but you are required to return your warrant card and you are placed on unpaid leave for the period of time that the career break is authorised. You can have anything from two months up to five years, but you have to qualify as they won't just let you take a break for the sake of it and definitely won't allow you to take a break to forge another career!

The process went something like this...

The application is submitted and then goes to HR, who have to read it and then send it out to the Divisional Inspector who then has to sanction it, and usually never supports applications for a career break as the inspector at that time was really old school. He then has to send it to the superintendent with supporting comments for approval. The superintendent will appraise the application and either support it or not, depending on what mood they are in on the day!

The whole process takes months and then when it's approved, and the date is agreed, you have to begin clearing your workload, handing back kits, and trying your hardest not to get injured on duty before you leave to begin the break!

In my case, it took about six weeks from application to my final shift, and like a true, devoted officer, an hour before I left work to begin my break I was still attending violent domestics and arresting people to the very last minute.

It was 23:30 and my final shift had come to an end. My team had bought me a watch and had a great leaving card made for me. I handed back my kit, protective vest, utility belt, CS spray, radio, baton, and handcuffs. I removed my Taser and locked it securely in the safe; the final item to hand over was my warrant card. That was hard I was always proud to serve as an officer and always had my warrant card with me, even when I was off duty. It never left me and I felt remorseful as this seemed so very final. I knew there would be no more camaraderie with my teammates, no more silly humour, no more watching over my colleague's backs in violent situations and vice versa, and no more banter in the crew room. I knew, at this point, it would be unlikely that I would wear the uniform again. I was proud to have served and proud to have been awarded two medals, one of which came with a signed letter from the Prime Minister, David Cameron, thanking me for my efforts in providing the Security for the 2012 Olympic Games. A nice keepsake for my children.

That was it. I walked out feeling exposed. I was, for all intents and purposes, a civilian, but I had an immense feeling of excitement, because in two days I was about to begin my property course that later became one of the best decisions I had ever made.

"Ladies and gentlemen, a really warm welcome to you all and thank you for giving up three days to spend with us in Birmingham..." Lorraine and I sat somewhere in the middle of a very packed room. We were at a nice round table with lots of other starry-eyed people. We were poised and ready to take in all the learning and education the next three days were about to offer. I had to make this work; I had to. I no longer had any income at all and only had about £15,000 in the bank, which was our life savings and that had to last me at least eighteen months. The worst-case scenario would be that I would have to return to the police, but that wasn't going to happen. I was determined, and I needed to make this work for my family.

"Ladies and gents, please give a massive welcome to the stage..." The crowd began clapping, and the energy in the room was high; we were all very excited as we were about to begin our education.

It was a large room and we were all sat cabaret-style. The trainer came on and introduced himself and there we were; our new chapter had begun.

During the first day, we learned how to find what a good property deal looked like for us and how much we needed to replace our income. For us, that was my salary which equated to a take-home of £1,800 a month by the time I had paid my pension and tax, National Insurance, and a little bit to charity each month. To be honest, I felt that was a decent living. Our costs were relatively low, so we set a target of £2,000 per month through property, and that felt like a lot!

By the time our second day came, we were excited about pushing forward with our new learning, albeit I was a little jaded after drinking too much wine in the bar with Lorraine the previous evening while brainstorming our new ideas.

We had already decided on our strategy. It was definitely Houses in Multiple Occupation (HMOs), but we were very clear that we wanted professional tenants and we were going to invest in Worcestershire.

While sipping our wine in the bar on the first night, Lorraine and I were scouring through Right Move and Zoopla (with the odd Facebook update and selfie). We came across a nice five-bedroom house, just outside of Worcester city centre with a private driveway and a double garage.

The only thing going against it was the location, as it was directly in front of Worcester City Football Club! The property was on the market for £187,000; the floor plans looked great, and it had already had extra bedrooms converted in the attic. If we changed the living room then we would get six bedrooms. It seemed perfect.

At this time in Worcester, we had no planning restrictions (I will cover this later in the book), which meant that we could convert the house into a small HMO (no more than six sleeping people) under Permitted Development. It also required a Mandatory HMO Licence.

We called the agent on our lunch break the following day and organised a viewing for the day after the course.

We thoroughly enjoyed our three days of property training, and it changed our mindset to see that there could be life beyond the police. It was all very exciting!

We also realised that we wanted more knowledge and accountability going forward. We knew that we could enroll on a twelve-month programme, which would probably give us the accountability that we were looking for. The only thing holding us back was the fact that it would have taken all of our savings, and we would have left us to live off Lorraine's salary. What the hell though; we are only here once, right?

We enrolled and decided that our chosen strategy would be HMOs (Houses in Multiple Occupation) rather than standard Buy to Let. Here's why.

## Why Choose HMOs?

We were looking for high cash flow so I could leave the police as soon as possible and, with HMOs, we would purchase several income streams at once. For example, a six-bedroom property would bring six income streams at once, as each bedroom is an income stream (rather than a single-let house). The great thing is, it doesn't have to actually need six bedrooms in the true sense of the word! A four-bedroom house, with a great living room and a dining room and large kitchen, would be perfect. We could use the kitchen as the communal area and simply turn the living room and dining room into bedrooms!

With six separate streams of income, if we have a void or if a tenant stops paying, we still have five streams left.

We always have a rule of thumb: we won't take on any property that doesn't lend itself to having at least five bedrooms, and the profit must be a minimum of £500 net per month per property. This takes into consideration an allowance for voids of 10% off the gross monthly rent and a maintenance cost of 5% off the gross monthly rent. We will cover this in more depth later in the deal stacking section.

We always look for a minimum of 15% Return on Investment, (ROI) per property.

## Comparison – Single-Let Property

We like to keep things simple, right? So for ease of reference, let's say you had a property worth £150,000. You purchase it at 75% Loan to value (LTV); we will need the correct mortgage product for the house. Again, we will look into that in more depth later, but for now, let's say that the interest rate on this mortgage is 6% (commercial). That may sound a little expensive, but it allows for any increase.

Based on this example, you would need to put in a deposit of £37,500 the monthly mortgage cost would be £562.50 (interest only) per month. You would need to pay stamp duty at the higher level as this will be an investment property at £5,000, legal fees of around £1,000, the property may or may not need a light refurb say £3,000. If you do need to extensively refurbish the property, you may need approval from the mortgage provider, so it's very important that you get the correct product and speak with a professional mortgage broker. The total estimated cost per month would be around £650, which would consist of the mortgage and the insurance, as the tenant would pay the bills as a single let property.

Let's presume that the monthly rent for this house would be £845. That would leave you with a staggering £195 per month profit before tax!

Does that sound like a good deal to you? Possibly. I guess it depends on what works for you, right?

The Return On Investment figure (ROI) for this deal would be:-

Annual Profit = £195 per month x 12 = £2,340 we then divide this figure by the total investment into the deal, in this case, it would be the deposit of £37,500, the legal fees of £1,000, the stamp duty of £5,000, and the refurb of £3,000 so the total money invested would be £46,500.

Annual profit £2,340 / Initial investment £46,500 x 100
= 5.03% ROI Is that a good deal for you?

## But with an HMO deal....

Remember we said that we purchase five (or more) income streams at once?

It's the same house, and for ease, we are presuming that we have no planning restrictions. (To be covered later.)

Property purchased at 150k
Refurb £15,000
Stamp Duty £5,000
Legal Cost £1,000
Deposit £37,500
Five bedrooms achieving £400 each =£2,000 pcm
Allowing 10% Voids = £200
Allowing 5% Maintenance = £100
Mortgage £562 @ 6%
Utilities £350
Profit £2,000 - £1,212 = £788 pcm £9,456 per year

## ROI

Annual Profit £9,456
/ Total investment £58,500
x 100
= 16.16% ROI

Now is that a better deal or is that a better deal?

You can see that everything here fits in with our benchmark: we have great cash flow and anything over £500 works, and we have a great ROI. Anything over 15% works for us.

Remember, we have factored in voids too, so if you don't have any, even better!

Personally, I only buy for cash flow and not for capital growth. If the property does go up in value, then that's the icing on the cake for us.

Not long after we booked the appointment, off we went to view our first property (that we sourced from Zoopla while in the bar drinking wine on our course). It wasn't far from where we lived and just on the outskirts of the city. We were met with the agent and the vendor.

The property was an end terrace with a very large driveway and ample parking for about four to five cars. The house itself was in relatively good condition. It had two small already converted loft bedrooms at the very top of the house and three nice bedrooms on the middle floor, with a living room and separate dining room downstairs and kitchen with a small utility room.

We had no planning restrictions at this point and we knew we would be able to turn this house into a small, six-bedroom HMO under permitted development taking the use from Planning class C3 (Dwelling House) to Planning class C4 (Small house of multiple occupation).

The vendor was a lovely man, but was getting on in years and, unfortunately, had begun to suffer from dementia which meant he needed full-time care and that was the reason he was selling. The asking price was £187,000, which wasn't particularly under market value at the time, but as I mentioned earlier, the property was situated directly in front of Worcester City Football Club. We had also been made aware that Worcester City FC were about to be relegated and they were looking to sell their pitch!

Lorraine and I went back to our office (our dining room at home) and discussed this purchase. We worked out our numbers and decided that this seemed like the perfect property for us to start with. It was a great location, and it had what would be six good size rooms, and it had ample parking space. All we needed to do was create a second bathroom and a spare WC with washbasin. The new bathroom could be fitted into the current utility room and the spare toilet into the cellar, so we decided to put in an offer. I called the agent and offered £177,000, feeling pleased with myself. I felt that I had a great chance at this price and our investing could now begin.

An hour later, my phone rang and I knew it was the agent. I went a crimson-red colour, and my heart was beating fast as I answered: "Mr Gannon?"

"Yes, speaking."

"Hi, I spoke to the vendor and he won't accept anything less than the asking price I'm afraid," and before he had a chance to finish his sentence, I said, "Ok, I'll offer the full asking price." I have no idea where this came from; it was my inner "Chimp" that decided offering the full asking price on a property that wasn't below market value was a great idea!

"Fantastic," the agent replied, "so before I go back to the vendor what is your situation regarding finance?"

"Finance?" I replied.

"Yes, do you have proof of funding?"

"Yes, of course," I stated with a very high-pitched squeaky voice!

"Great, so if you could email that to me and I will put the offer forward to the vendor."

Shit! I didn't have proof of funds! Why the hell did I say that I did?? Oh man, he really caught me on the hop with that one, and there I was, standing with my pants down! (Metaphorically speaking).

Five minutes later the phone went again. I looked and saw the number. It was the agent again: "Rick Gannon," I answered in what I felt like was an even more squeaky voice.

"Hi, Mr Gannon. It's Lee again. I have great news. The vendor has accepted your offer!"

"Brilliant," I replied feeling a little sick inside, "so, if you could get the proof of funds over, and the details of your solicitor, we can draft up a memorandum of sale."

We ended the conversation and I felt terrible. What had I just done? I had just agreed to buy a property for £187,000 with what? My police medals?

# Chapter 5
# I Have a Great Opportunity for You

I was tucking into my chicken Madras which, by now, had become a regular Friday night ritual at our local Balti house. Lorraine and I were having dinner with Lorraine's parents and our kids. A few cans of cider into the evening, I just blurted out to my father-in-law, "Hey, you know that pension money that you just got? Well, I have an amazing opportunity for you!" "Oh really?" came my father-in-law's sceptical response, "what's that then?" I could sense the doubt in his voice.

I explained that we had found this great house and we were going to turn it into an HMO and make an absolute fortune. As I'm sure you can imagine, my father-in-law was a little dubious, but as the night went on, and we had both consumed a large amount of Madras and alcohol, we had agreed on business terms on the back of a beer mat!

My father-in-law had, in principle, agreed to lend us all of the money for the deposit to purchase the house and all of the money to do the refurbishment in return for a 50% share of the equity and a 50% share of the monthly profit. We were in business!

I now had proof of funds, and my father-in-law and I took out a joint mortgage to buy the house. We were about to embark on our very first HMO. It was very exciting.

Over the next few weeks, I began with my due diligence and contacted the council who were very helpful indeed. They gave me all the information I needed, with legislation to help in obtaining my licence. Now, I needed to find a great building team.

I did what most would do at this point and went online and searched "builders in Worcester". I called five people asking for quotes and sat and waited, and waited…and eventually two people called me back and made appointments. Things were moving forward.

"Hello, it's Rick Gannon. We had a meeting at 5pm tonight at the house?"

"Ah, yeah, sorry kidda. Can't make it tonight I got held up with summat."

Great! So now I'm down to one builder who was due at six, so let's hope he turns up!

Six o'clock arrived, and sure enough builder number two turned up in a little white Renault van. He jumped out of it and came straight over.

"Rick, is it?"

"Yes, hi."

"Great, well I know all about HMOs as I have three of my own. Don't know why you're bothering to be honest as mine are always empty! Nevertheless, I'm keeping them for the kids as an investment."

Now, I'm no builder, but I felt it a bit odd that this chap had no notebook and no tape measure – and even I know if you are a builder you always have a tape measure. As we walked around the house, this man continued to kick the skirting boards and tap the walls rather annoyingly with his index finger. I blurted out, "Don't you need to measure up and write this all down?"

"I don't need a book mate," was his flippant reply as he got out his trusty index finger and began tapping the side of his head, "Got this you see."

'Oh bollocks,' was my initial thought. Back to the drawing board.

The following week was our local property investors' meeting, you know the sort, and I'm guessing as you are reading this book you have already been to at least one or two. Well, for those that have, you will relate to this. For those that haven't, get along to one as you're missing a really valuable resource!

During the meeting, everyone in the room gets the opportunity to stand up for a few seconds and introduce themselves to tell everyone else why they are there. Most won't stand up (again a total waste and if that's you maybe don't bother going next time) It was my turn. I had nothing planned but public speaking never really phased me. "Hi, I'm Rick, and I have just begun investing in HMOs in Worcester, and I really need a building team to help put my latest project together. If you know anyone that can help, then please come and see me at the break."

A large, well-built man then stood up and announced, "I am a builder, and I specialise in HMO conversions all around the country." Now you can see the power of networking. Not only did everyone else know why I was there, but I now had a contact for a specialist HMO builder.

This is one of the reasons I bang on to people on my mentoring programme to network your butt off in the first twelve months. If your net isn't cast, then you will catch no fish.

This man became my very first builder and went on to complete my first two HMO Projects to an excellent standard.

In full credit to our builder, we had no time to waste as we had Article 4 planning direction looming around the corner and to gain Grandfather Rights we needed the property converted to the required standards. A licence then needed to be applied for, and the property needed to be tenanted by at least three people from two separate families BEFORE Article 4 Direction came into place more on Article 4 later.

Fortunately, due to my proactive marketing, we sold every room while the property was under construction and managed to get the property fully tenanted before Article 4 Direction was introduced.

It was tight though, and our builder and his team were literally applying the final coat of gloss paint to the back utility room as the first tenant was knocking on the front door to check in!

## Case Study Deal 1

The house was a 1960's end of terrace. It had five bedrooms, a living room, a dining room, a driveway, and a double garage. It was a big house that didn't need too much work done to it.

It did have some down points. It had an old pub next door as a neighbour and it was directly in front of Worcester City Football Club. The asking price was £187,000. We were shown around by the agent and met the vendor who was an elderly gent who was about to go into sheltered accommodation.

We could see that the property would make a great six-bedroom HMO just by simply converting the front living room into a bedroom and by making some slight adjustments in order to obtain our licence. The location, although not ideal, was just outside the city centre and it had private parking.

We were also very aware that we were only about four months away from Worcester City Council bringing in Article 4 Planning Direction. (Covered later)

## Case Study

- Property sourced via EA for £187,000.
- JV partner put all the money in for the deposit to purchase AND the refurb
- I managed and sourced the tenants
- Both received 50% of the monthly net profit
- Both received 50% of the capital growth
- Purchased on a 75/25 mortgage (Always get the correct product)
- Deposit required £46,750

- Refurb required £20,000
- Stamp Duty £1,500 (before the increase)
- Legal cost £1,000
- Total money into the deal £69,250 all from Joint Venture partner
- Six rooms at an average £361 average per room = £2,166 (at the time)
- Voids and maintenance 15% = £324.9
- Mortgage and bills circa £1,000
- Total bills £1,324.9
- Total cash flow £2,166 – £1,324.9 = £841.1 profit
- £420 per month each
- JV partner achieves 7.3% ROI instead of 1.5% he was achieving in the bank
- JV partner also has 50% of any capital growth in the property

Remember that I said earlier "What if it all goes wrong?" Well, we did indeed refinance this deal two years later for a staggering £260,000 on an 85% LTV HMO mortgage product which meant we made £80,750 back! This paid all the £69,250 back to my father-in-law, and we had £11,500 in profit which we split 50/50.

Now, we both had 50% equity and 50% of the net cash flow and a FREE house! Now is that a good deal?

I have since learned to stop thinking about, 'what if it goes wrong?' and I began to think, 'what if it goes right?'

We now had a business! At least we had one house, but every marathon begins with a single step! I guess we now needed to set up the business structure.

# Chapter 6
# Getting it Right

T he first thing that I suggest you do when setting up your company is talk to a Property Tax Specialist and take advice on how to do this correctly, i.e. Limited Company vs Sole Trader etc.

Trust me, this will pay massive dividends going forward and it's always better to start with the end in mind. When we started investing, we took advice from someone who told us it would be better to have an individual bank account for each house. As we were inexperienced, we did exactly that. Little did we know, three years later we would still be unravelling the mess that we had created in doing this. Choose carefully who you take advice from. Like anything, you get what you pay for and the cheapest definitely isn't the best. Most specialist Property Tax Advisors will come at a premium, but they will save you a fortune by giving the correct advice. Ask yourself this, would you take your Ferrari to a Mini garage for a service?

Once we had decided on company structure and a company name, which incidentally was New Era Property Solutions Limited, we decided to get all the back office stuff done first.

We needed stationery and business cards and, of course, a website. I went to town on this straight away, ordering business cards from VistaPrint on the internet, which is very easy, then I began to build a website myself. There are lots of website developers and website software out there, but please be careful on how much you spend at this stage. You need to have an internet presence and it needs to look professional, but if you do choose to have one built for you, I wouldn't recommend spending more than £1,000 at this point. You can build on it as you grow.

We had our stationery, our cards had arrived, and we were poised to open several (unnecessary) bank accounts. The next thing we needed was a telephone answering service. We wanted to create a professional image when people called and reasoned that it would be better than giving a mobile telephone number out. The great thing about a call answering service is that you can get your mind into focus and be "in the room" when you call them back. It also gives you the opportunity to research the property before you make the call.

There are lots of call answering services available; just Google them.

Next, we needed an accounts package. Even though, at this point, we didn't have much property, we knew it was better to get this done at the beginning and to start with the end in mind. We chose a package called Xero, which is great for small business startups and doesn't cost much per month.

TIP: You will need to register with a Property Redress Scheme such as 'The Property Ombudsman' or the 'Property Redress Scheme' as soon as you begin collating personal data from tenants. You must also register for data protection with The Information Commissioners Office www.ico.org

**Deal Stacking:**

**ROI**

The ROI (Return on Investment) is calculated by taking your annual Profit divided by the total amount of money required to be put into the deal x 100.

What sort of ROI would you be comfortable with? I guess this is highly individual. Some banks, at the moment, are offering up to a staggering 1.5%, and that's pretty high, but usually you can expect around 0.5%. I am being facetious, of course.

In the early stages of our investing career, we worked on anything between 10%-20% return and upwards as that worked for us. We knew we could achieve this, although we now stick to anything above 20%.

**Mortgage calculations:**

It's always important to stress test your mortgage to 6% upwards. Most products, at the time of writing, are below this figure. If we factor in every eventuality then it future proofs the deal and allows for contingency. Choose a good broker preferably one that is also a property investor and understands the industry with access to the whole of the market. It's very important that you choose the correct product for the building, and you must always inform the broker of your intentions.

There are products for just about everything, including bridging finance, so whatever it is you choose to do with the property, be sure to disclose it.

## Insurance:

Another product that is largely overlooked is insurance; you must get the correct product for the property. I very often see investors and landlords go for the cheapest product and find only, to their horror, when they attempt to make a claim that they are not covered. Cheapest isn't best! Make sure that you are covered for every eventuality. There are some great products out there that will cover full liability for the whole cost of the house in the event of malicious damage, i.e. arson. They will also insure loss of rent, and this will include re-housing the tenant should you need to. Always shop around and make sure you choose a broker that understands the market.

## Voids and maintenance

It's fair to say that, at some point, your property may have empty rooms, and we need to make sure we account for this in the deal stacking process.

We always allow for 10% off the gross monthly rent for voids.

We also allow for 5% off the gross monthly rent for maintenance.

## Utilities

We provide all-inclusive bills in all of our HMOs. We find that the Tenants prefer this as they can budget easily and don't have the hassle of managing anything more than their monthly rent.

The cost of this differs per property. Many utility companies will assist you with this and give you a fixed fee per person per house, but this comes at a cost as it's also the service you are paying for.

## Council Tax

If you are renting to students, then you will be Council Tax exempt for the period that your property is occupied. If you have periods between tenancies, then you will be responsible for paying the Council Tax during that time. You will have to provide the council with proof of each student. Usually, the university will issue them with a Council Tax exemption certificate.

If you are renting to anyone other than students, then the property will be charged for Council Tax. We also factor this into our costs and pay this on the tenant's behalf. Usually for us, in our area a six-bedroom property costs on average around £150 per month.

## Stamp Duty

Use a great stamp duty calculator. (Just search online) If this is a second property, then you will have to pay considerably more, a very important part of the deal stacking process.

## Due Diligence

Make sure you follow the below steps to pick the correct investing area that suits your strategy. Conducting the correct due diligence before you commit to buying or renting any property is paramount. It is the difference between making or losing money.

Let's start here:

**Investing area:**

It's absolutely key that you get this right so choose carefully.

When we began investing in HMOs, we wanted to take over the world. I was happy to invest from Lands' End to John O'Groats and everywhere in between! Fortunately for us, the reality hit very quickly that HMOs are not 100% passive and they take a lot of work getting set up.

Important things to consider are legislation in the area:

Does the area have any restrictions which may prevent you from turning a house into an HMO? If it does, you need to find out before you waste your time looking.

Article 4 planning direction, "Article 4 what?" I hear you crying.

Ok, get a pen and a piece of paper because you need to get this stuff right. If you don't, then you will waste your time and your money.

Article 4 planning direction has absolutely nothing to do with Licensing, so let's get that out of the way first. I'm going to say that again. Article 4 planning has absolutely nothing to do with Licensing of any form. Got it? Good! If not, read this again until you are confident you understand it.

**Article 4 planning direction**

An Article 4 planning direction is made by the local planning authority. It restricts the scope of permitted development rights either in relation to a particular area or site, or a particular type of development anywhere in the authority's area.

Where an A4 direction is in effect, a planning application may be required for development that would otherwise have been permitted development. Article 4 directions are used to control works that could threaten the character of an area of acknowledged importance such as a conservation area.

If you have A4 direction in your area in connection with HMOs, you will be required to submit a planning application. Article 4 direction doesn't always mean you can't invest in that area, it just means that it may be a little harder!

Most councils will have certain criteria that will need to be met. In my area, no more than 10% HMO is permitted within a 100-metre radius, and if there is already an HMO next door, then you may be disqualified. We also have to provide off-road parking.

The other way you can obtain an HMO in an A4 area would be to purchase or take over a property that has already been given permission or has been afforded "Grandfather Rights". This means that if they were already operating as an HMO before the start of the legislation, then they are permitted to continue. But always do your due diligence and obtain proof. This may come in the form of a certificate of lawful use or AST contracts / licences dated prior to the introduction of the direction.

## Licensing

This is NOT planning. Remember that this is totally separate. There is nothing to say that you can't obtain a licence in any property, provided that you adhere to the guidelines and that you are a fit and proper person, (and you pay the fee of course) but without the necessary planning consent, your licence will be useless.

## Mandatory HMO Licensing

Your property will be required to be licensed under this scheme if it meets the following criteria:

You have five or more tenants over three or more storeys, forming two separate families with shared facilities.

Simple enough to understand, but there is a caution here. At the time of writing this book, it has been announced that in 2018 there may be an amendment to this, and it is likely that this will change to 5 tenants over 1 or more storeys may require a Mandatary HMO Licence.

I believe that this is a positive introduction and regulates the industry to a higher standard and, therefore, will force out any rogue landlords trying to operate "under the radar."

You will need to check this legislation for yourself to confirm the current position.

## Additional / selective licensing

Some councils have gone one step further and have adopted additional and selective licensing schemes, which means if you have an HMO, (three or more people from two separate families with shared facilities) then you may require a licence regardless. Once again, this will be up to you to check this with your local council. Also to point out here that some councils may require you as the Landlord to be licensed too!

Always contact your council as a part of your due diligence to ascertain which scheme they adopt. Mandatory licences are not transferable.

## Location

It is key! We start from the town centre and work our way out from there. Tenants like to have everything close by such as shops, bars, supermarkets, and gyms.

The closest to the train station as possible; this allows more flexibility to the tenant.

You don't necessarily need city centre properties, but start from that location and work outwards. As long as the property is close to a bus/transport route, then it shouldn't be a problem.

Pick a nice safe area for your house, rightfully so we should be offering safe accommodation. You can check the local crime statistics on the internet.

## Supply / Demand

Obviously, this is a big factor in any deal stacking, as without the tenants, we don't have a business. Always research the area and check the tenant demand.

Check the supply-demand level by looking on websites such as spareroom.co.uk on here you can check the buttons and see how many rooms are available in the area against how many tenants are searching. This will also give you a great idea of how much rent to charge, and what the local competition is doing.

Call the local agents and tell them you are an investor and you are researching the area. You will find them very accommodating.

If you are looking to house students, then you will need to be investing close to universities, but be aware as universities will usually house first-year students themselves and, in some cases, may even offer accommodation after the first year. Make contact with the university housing officer and ask what the situation is. Some universities will offer you a guaranteed rent scheme and take over the management of your property.

Local blue-chip businesses also offer a great avenue for filling rooms, as do hospitals. We will cover marketing rooms later in the book.

Obtaining the correct property and being compliant. In  my experience vanilla, mid-terrace townhouses work the best. They are like a Tardis and seem to go on forever, we look for:

Properties that can be converted to a minimum of five bedrooms. That doesn't mean we are looking for five-bedroom houses, but as long as we can rearrange the internal structure to suit this. It could mean you buy a three-bedroom house with an integral garage, a lounge, kitchen, and dining room. You can convert the integral garage (under permitted development) and then convert the living room or the dining room into a bedroom. You will now have five bedrooms and a communal area.

Room sizes are key here so you must ensure that you comply with the minimum room sizes for your area which, for us, are currently 6.52sm for single occupancy and 10.2sm for double occupancy. This is our council minimum standards and you need to be aware that some councils will add to this and may even require more, sometimes significantly. Always call your housing team at the council and establish your local regulations. Best practice would be to invite your HMO Officer to any prospective property you may have to establish their opinion and offer you any advice to convert the property to the required standards. By doing this, it may save you a huge amount of money by not converting the property to the correct required standards. In most cases, you may have to pay the HMO Officer to conduct the visit, but this will be worth every penny.

Parking may be a requirement in your area. For example, we have to provide three off-road spaces for a five-bedroom HMO. (But we do have article 4 planning direction).

Kitchens will need to be big enough for each tenant to have a least one private cupboard each. You may also need two hobs subject to your local council requirements.

You will also be required to provide enough bathrooms and toilets for your tenants. In a shared six-bedroom house, we have to provide two separate bathrooms and two toilets. One of the toilets needs to be separate from both bathrooms. This is pretty standard, but again you will need to check with your council what their requirements are.

Irrespective of licensing, you will be required to ensure your properties are safe from fire. You will be required to have 30min fire doors on each risk room and an automatic door closer with a smoke seal around the door.

You will need a suitable fire/smoke detection system. If you don't know which one, then refer to the "Lacors" guidelines. The system will need to be tested in accordance with these guidelines by a competent person and serviced regularly by a qualified engineer. A certificate will need to be issued.

Emergency lighting will need to be provided for any complex escape route. This will also need to be tested and serviced regularly.

Fire extinguishers may need to be provided. This is subject to your local council.

The property will need an electrical testing certificate, which lasts five years and will then need to be re-tested.

All Gas appliances will need to be tested annually, and a certificate will need to be obtained.

Every Council will have a document called something like "Amenities Standards for HMOs" this document will detail all the minimum required standards that your property will need to meet. You should be able to go onto your council website and download it as a pdf.

Almost as soon as we completed on our first deal, we were about to go away on holiday. (Bad timing I know). So we handed the keys over to our builder (the one we sourced at the meeting) to begin the refurbishment.

## Refurbishing the house to the required legal standard:

The below is a list of the conversion work we had done to our first HMO property.

New fire doors (FD30) on all risk areas which were the kitchen, the cellar, the living room, and all the bedrooms. The doors needed top closers and intumescent smoke strips and new fireproof door frames to ensure fire safety.

Supply and fit Euro cylinder thumb turn locks on each bedroom door and both the front and back doors to the house. These are designed to escape from a fire without needing a key. If you use the old standard, Yale locks, these will cause you a huge problem with tenants locking themselves out on a regular basis. Yale now does a great Roller Bolt type system that prevents this. Regardless of which one you use, make sure they are designed so tenants can't lock themselves out, but can escape safely in the event of a fire.

Installation of a Cat. A Fire Alarm system as this was a Bedsit type HMO. Lacors advises that if you operate a Bedsit type HMO which means the Tenants are not likely to know each other and they have signed a separate AST agreement, then a Cat. A system with a panel and call points is required. If your property is a Shared House type HMO which means that you let the property to a group of friends on 1 AST, then Lacors recommend you install a Cat. D mains interlinked smoke detection system. No panel is required, with a sensor and sounder in each bedroom, one on the landing and one in the hallway, kitchen, cellar and a heat detector in the kitchen with an interlinked carbon-monoxide detector in the boiler room.

Installation of an emergency lighting system to include four lights in total. A digital TV point in each bedroom. (We still do this.)

Hardboard flooring under the carpets in all sleeping rooms that prevent the ingress of smoke through any possible gaps in the floor from below rooms. New downstairs shower room and toilet. (Building regs required).

New consumer unit and some rewiring and testing and certifying of the house electrics. (Building regs required).

Painting of the whole house, which consisted of six bedrooms, a living room, kitchen, and two bathrooms.

Fortunately, we didn't need a new kitchen, and the carpets were brand new!

Testing and certification of the gas boiler.

Please check your local council's requirements when it comes to kitchen space.

# Chapter 7
# Onwards and Upwards

I was a little apprehensive as I left to go on holiday. This was our first project and it needed to be right! It was in good hands though.

During my holiday, I was regularly updated with progress over text messages with photos; the team did a great job of keeping me well-informed. I was able to enjoy my holiday with my family without any issues.

After two glorious weeks in the sun with my family, we returned to the UK. No sooner was I off the plane than I went straight to the house to check on the progress. Remember, I was on a tight deadline with this as Article 4 planning direction was looming and I needed to be awarded Grandfather Rights.

I only had a few months to get the property passed for licensing and tenanted with a minimum of three individuals from two separate families to claim the rights. No pressure!

Progress was good and the house a hive of activity; everything seemed to be on schedule.

As the work continued, I began to market the property online in an attempt to gain a waiting list for the rooms. Even though it was still effectively a building site, I needed to be proactive, and I suggest you do the same. Tenants will actually reserve rooms while the house is under refurbishment. They will buy into the vision.

We were lucky that one of the bigger bedrooms had been painted and was almost ready, although the rest of the house was a work in progress. We placed a bed in the one room, hung a picture on the wall, dressed it with a nice colourful set of bedding, and photographed it with my iPhone. This then formed the basis of my first advert on www.spareroom.co.uk

I was very conscious on timings, so I wanted my advert to stand out from the others.

*"Amazing Double Room Close to the City."*

*"We are looking for a clean and respectful person to share our lovely newly-refurbished professional house close to the city centre.*

*"The house is in a lovely quiet location with a private driveway and private ample parking; the rooms are all-inclusive of bills.*

*The location is fantastic, the property is the end of terrace in a small block of four private houses and is in walking distance to the city centre, and two minutes from the train station."*

*"Both the room and the house are fully furnished to a very high standard. The room benefits from a brand new double bed and mattress, a wardrobe, chest of drawers, bedside table, and a desk and chair. I can also include a brand new duvet and bed linen, if required."*

*"The house has super-fast Fibre Optic Broadband and a digital TV point in every bedroom."*

*"The property has a great communal living room which boasts a wall-mounted flat-screen digital TV, two x leather reclining couches, a coffee table and a dining table. The house also has two fitted shower rooms and toilets."*

*"Outside, there is a private driveway with ample parking for six cars and a lovely private patio area to enjoy a glass of wine or a cold beer after a stressful day at work! It also has a brick built BBQ for those hot summer nights."*

*"The communal rooms will be cleaned regularly at no extra cost, and all bills, council tax, water, gas, electricity, TV licence (in the communal room) and Wi-Fi are included in the rent. There are no hidden costs. The monthly rental figure is all you pay."*

*"Please contact me if you are interested. It really is an amazing house, so hurry! If you are in full-time professional employment and you are serious about living in a high standard house with like-minded housemates, then please give me a call."*

*"Sorry, but this room is not available for couples, DHSS or students. NO DEPOSIT."*

*"We are private landlords."*

That was my first ever advert! We have enhanced this many times over the years, but we had great success with this. Please feel free to use it as an example.

We decided, at the beginning, that we would not charge deposits, as we wanted to be head and shoulders above the rest of the competition and we were operating our own portfolio, then the risk was solely our own.

This also meant that we didn't have to take an inventory when checking tenants in and out of the property as we had no redress, so it would have been pointless. The other thing to consider here: we choose only to take professional tenants, so in theory, the risk level was relatively low and I'm pleased to report that we have only ever had to replace one soiled mattress in the history of the company, as nothing else has been damaged or stolen.

The response rate to our advert was amazing, and I began taking bookings almost immediately. But before showing anyone the room, I did stipulate that this was a house still under refurbishment and wouldn't be ready for about four to six weeks. That didn't seem to put anyone off and the viewings started! (Hard hats and high vis. jackets at the ready)

My first viewing was about to take place. It was a young, male bank manager who had been promoted and needed to move into the area quickly. He was prepared to rent a hotel room in the interim period. He loved the room that had been decorated and could see the rest of the house taking shape. He came to view it with his dad and reserved it straight away! He took away with him our paper application form to complete and send back for referencing.

That was my very first viewing! Wow, what a feeling. This had a great impact on my confidence and I knew that this was going to work well. He later fed back that he had seen lots of rooms, but was impressed at my professionalism.

The enquiries continued to roll in, followed by two remote enquires from two girls, currently living in France. They said they wanted to take the rooms without viewing (owing to the location). I sent over the contracts via email and they arrived back to me five days later! The first contract from the bank manager was now also signed, so within two weeks I had sold all the rooms!

Now you may have also experienced this feeling. If not, I hope you soon will as it is a paradigm shift from, "What if it goes wrong?" to "Shit, this is actually working."

So we had now sold all the rooms, and dates were set for everyone to move in. There's nothing like a deadline to keep the building team motivated. (That and a KFC family bucket.)

I will never forget the panic to this day, as my first two tenants from France were arriving at the property, and I still had the whole building team painting and tiling the new bathroom! The gloss paint was literally still wet in the whole house.

The front doorbell rang and, sure enough, my new French tenants were standing there all happy and smiling with suitcases in hand as the builders left by the back kitchen door! Now that was a tight deadline!

That was it. We now had an HMO and we had every room filled with: two ladies who had moved from France, a bank manager, a sports psychologist, a factory manager, and a police civilian support worker. All six contracts signed well before the Article 4 direction cut-off date and, most importantly, we started to get money into the bank. I now had a thirst I needed to quench!

I remember sitting up all night on the 30th into the 1st of the month watching the rent drop into my bank account. It was a great feeling!

"I would like to buy it – but not for two years – and in the meantime, I would like to rent it."

We were looking at a lovely mid-terrace property in the city centre, literally one street away from the main train station. We had seen the property for sale on Rightmove and we still had several months before the looming Article 4 planning direction was to be introduced. It was going to be tight, but we were laser-focused and we had a thirst!

The property was empty and it was owned by a nice man that, unfortunately, had recently lost his wife. The house had been used to foster young children and each room had its own sink. There were four bedrooms, a living room, a lounge, and a kitchen with a separate toilet in the back. I can't really explain it, but although the house was empty, I could feel the positive energy inside. The feeling continued as we walked into the rear garden, where I noticed seashells placed strategically between the flowers and small homemade garden decorations were hanging from the trees. I could just see, in my mind, the children playing in the garden with their temporary parents. Even as I sit here writing this now, the warm feeling comes back to and makes the hairs stand up on my neck.

I had to have it. You know when something just feels right? Well, this was one of those moments, and, fortunately for us, the agent that showed us around was a very articulate postgraduate, and he was hungry for a deal as much as we were. He understood our offer straight away and replied with, "Oh, so you want to do a lease option?"

"Well yes, if possible," I replied, feeling quite shocked that he even knew what that was.

We were told that the owner had no mortgage outstanding on this property and the vendor didn't need the cash right away.

We went back to our dining room office and crunched some numbers. With a little bit of negotiating between the agent and the vendor, we agreed, in principle, to take the property on a Lease Purchase Option.

We would pay the estate agent fees up front, which were around £2,000, and we agreed on an eighteen-month lease with an option to purchase at the end of the lease. The vendor wouldn't allow any more than this, and to my surprise, he only asked for £500 a month in rent during each month during the lease period!

It did take a little bit of time to put this deal together, as the vendor insisted on having several face-to-face meetings with the agent just to ensure he knew and understood the proposal fully.

We were conscious of timings on this deal as Article 4 was getting closer and we really did need to move quickly. It required a similar refurb as our first HMO. I also needed to fill the rooms quickly.

Before we signed the legal documents, we managed to agree to a key undertaking, which meant the owner agreed to us having access to the house while the documents were being completed. This way, we could start things moving. The undertaking came with an agreement to begin works straight away with a provision that if the deal fell through we would have to make right any damage or alterations. We got the keys, and three hours later, the team were in to begin the conversion.

I didn't hang around. I marketed the rooms the same day using the photographs I had from our first project, which was now fully tenanted. I managed to fill the rooms in the new house within two weeks, all with professional tenants who bought into the vision, once again, that this was a brand new fully-refurbished house.

Deal number two was now secured, contracts were signed and tenants had been sourced. The last tenant moved in with only days to spare before the introduction of A4 Planning Direction.

We had made it! I had created eleven HMO rooms, all of which were fully occupied, and I had created an income of £1,400 net profit per month from absolutely nothing! I was one house away from being able to give up my job in the police, and I was only three months into the journey! My thirst was now stronger than ever!

# Chapter 8
# Lease Purchase Option and Marketing

W hat is a Lease Purchase Option? It is when you control a property under a legally binding lease agreement, which will allow you treat the property as your own during the term of the lease. It will allow you to let the rooms out on an individual basis as an HMO and during the term, you will pay the owner a pre-agreed monthly fee, which is usually around the single-let value of the property or slightly above.

We guarantee the monthly fee regardless of the property being occupied or not. This is a big risk, but also a huge motivator in making sure that we fill the rooms.

You will also have the "option to purchase", written within the options part of the agreement or as a separate stand-alone agreement, which will detail the fact that you have the "option" to purchase the property at a future pre-determined date at a fixed price. But note that this is an "option" to purchase, not an obligation, and means that at the end of the agreement you can walk away if you choose to.

Why would the seller allow this? With an LPO, we can offer over the current market value in the knowledge that the property is likely (but not guaranteed) to increase in value during the lease period. Therefore, it will be worth more in the future, which means that you are potentially purchasing a below market value property and the seller is also getting more than they would if they sold it in today's market. This would also work well if the seller is currently in negative equity, as they can make money each month on the rent you pay them and potentially they may also make a profit they wouldn't have had before when you buy at the fixed price in the future.

You may have heard the phrase "Buy a house for a pound" well this is exactly what this means. With this type of agreement, you will need to pay for the "consideration" of the lease, and this can be any amount. It can even be a peppercorn! Apparently, that's still a legally binding consideration, although I don't know of anyone ever having tested it! More often than not, it's either a pound or the first month's rent. It could even be the legal fees that you pay on the vendor's behalf.

There are several things that you will need to consider when adopting the Lease Purchase Option strategy.

Like anything we do, we have to remain ethical and transparent throughout the process. It is very important that the seller fully understands what that process is and the fact that it is an "option" to buy not an "obligation".

I recommend that the seller seeks independent legal advice. It may be proposed that they seek advice from a property specialist that understands these sort of deals. If they choose a general practice solicitor, there is a risk they may not understand the details and could advise their client not to go ahead.

If the seller does have a mortgage, then they will need consent to the lease and for the house to be traded as an HMO from their mortgage provider.

If the property is mortgaged, then it is in your interest to ensure that the owner of the property is servicing the mortgage correctly. This is in order to protect your investment, and there are a few ways that you can do this. You could pay the monthly mortgage on their behalf and send a statement to the owner each month as proof that you have done so. Some owners accept this and others don't. If they aren't happy with you doing this and, to be honest, I don't blame them, as they are pretty vulnerable if you then default on the payments. My other suggestion would be to ask them for a monthly or quarterly statement confirming that they are servicing the debt in the correct manner. That way you both have peace of mind. You can also have it written in your agreement that if the bank repossessed the property through negligence on the owner's part for not servicing the debt, then you shall not be held liable for any cost and the lease should be dissolved. You may then consider action against the owner to recover any loss of future income. Please seek legal advice regarding this.

The owner of the property will also need to ensure that they have the correct insurance cover in place for this type of an agreement. This is vital and we always ask for a copy of the policy to keep on file. This is something that the owner would have to undertake, but in my experience, some owners bury their heads in the sand and only take out straightforward Buy-to-Let Insurance which wouldn't be sufficient for a shared house/HMO.

## Exercising the option to purchase

Let's presume that you have been trading the house for a few years and the time has come where you either want to buy the property early on in the agreement or the agreement is nearing the end.

Please don't become unstuck here, and make sure that you have read and understand your lease and option agreement.

It is likely that the option agreement will require you to serve notice on the seller (owner) within a specific time frame for you to purchase the property at the agreed pre-determined price. Failure to serve this notice within the required time limit can make the agreement null and void, meaning the seller's legal requirement to sell the property to you at the agreed price may be removed. They could now take the property back from you resulting in you losing any money you have invested! Read the documents and understand them! If you have any doubt, take professional advice from your legal team.

## Financing your LPO at the end of the term.

It's important to make you aware that I am not a mortgage broker, nor am I a financial advisor, so I am not permitted to offer regulated advice, but I can share with you my opinion which is based on my experiences. Please note that you must always speak with a regulated professional to get the best possible advice on finance and current mortgage products. The paragraph that follows are my observations based on my own experiences and do not constitute advice.

There is a very important factor with Lease Purchase Options that most trainers fail to mention when the time comes to exercise your option and to purchase the property. So that you don't become disappointed, you need to be aware that it's likely you will only obtain funding for the agreed purchase price (the price you are paying) which is not necessarily going to be the same as the current market value. If your property has gone up considerably in value during the lease period, you may want to contact a broker to take advice on how to maximise on this uplifted value if you can.

Here is an example based on one of my recent Lease Purchase Options:

I agreed, two years ago, to buy this property with the future option purchase price of £193,000. I am now two years down the line and the property has risen in value during this time and is now worth £230,000.

This doesn't mean that I will be able to obtain traditional funding for the new price of £230,000 as I am buying it at £193,000. I am only able to get traditional funding for £193,000, the rest will sit as equity in the property until I can refinance in the future.

My options here could be:

- Traditional funding and leave the equity in the property.
- Bridging finance at true market value, then refinance with a traditional lender at a later stage. (Can be expensive).
- Cash purchase.

Start with the end in mind and please don't think that you will be given a mortgage five years in the future at the increased value. Remember you are only likely to get lending on the price that you are paying and no more. Always take professional advice from a regulated broker.

We were doing great, we were following the instructions given to us by our mentor and we now had two HMOs, one that we owned and one that was on a Lease Purchase Option that we would own in eighteen months' time.

A few months had passed by now, and we had the much-anticipated dreaded Article 4 planning direction introduced. I had to prove that both houses were occupied as HMOs before the direction and I was required to send off the Assured Shorthold Tenancy Agreements (AST's) for all the tenants in each of the houses to the local council to gain the necessary Grandfather Rights. This wasn't that bad, and I had been worrying about it unnecessarily. I sent over the information as per the instructions and I never heard anything back!

The first two houses were relatively easy as were we less restricted. But now we had A4 direction, we were going to need to up our game now we couldn't convert a house into an HMO under permitted development, and we would have to apply for planning permission for any conversion.

We could though begin marketing directly to the people that already owned HMOs to see if they would like to either sell or do a Rent-to-Rent or even an LPO. Like us, if they already had a converted HMO that was trading before the introduction of A4 then they would also be afforded Grandfather Rights.

We now had our first two properties and we were super-motivated as we knew that this worked for us and as we had just completed two HMOs, we knew that we could just rinse and repeat.

Our energy was high and we just knew this was going to work.

We revisited our marketing campaign as we wanted to give it everything we had. A very wise ex-colleague of mine from my policing days once said to me, "just spend five minutes extra on each task and that way your work will be far superior to everyone else's." I have adopted that philosophy ever since in everything I do.

Over the following nine months we attacked the market quite aggressively which proved very successful for us. Here are my top tips to help you with marketing and deal sourcing.

**Marketing and deal sourcing**

There are many ways to obtain property using tried and tested techniques and a few new ones too. Rather than list them all, (I seriously wouldn't have enough space in this book), I have written a separate book on deal sourcing called *"45 Ways to Buy Property". You can find this on Amazon.*

The following tips are my top ten deal sourcing strategies beginning with the most effective (in my experience) first.

Obtaining great property deals should be a fundamental core strategy for achieving your property-related goals. The problem is that you will get busy once you get one or two deals the real wealth-building strategy is to keep the flow of deals entering your funnel.

Remember if the deal is good you will always find the funds. The most common reason for being held back is the belief that you 'can't' find deals or the belief you 'can't' find the money to fund the deals you do have. Deals are everywhere, but you do have to look for them; they won't just fall into your lap. You have to take action. If you do find a good deal, then you won't have any problem finding the funds. Trust me, I'm an ex- policeman!

**Direct to vendor marketing letters. What are they?**

This is my all-time favourite of marketing strategies, as it's very directive and if you are positioned correctly, then it remains very effective!

Here's how we do it:

- Every council is required to publish a list of Licensed HMOs along with the name of the licence holder. Section 232 of the Housing Act states that any person can have access to that list at any reasonable time.
- Some councils are pretty protective with this list and don't publish it freely, but will allow you to visit their offices and view it or write it down. Other councils are more flexible and sometimes publish the list on their website for you to download as a PDF.
- Your aim is to obtain this list, as it will be the best-targeted marketing you will ever do and when you do get it treat it as your secret recipe!
- Remember that the people on the list are already licensed landlords with HMOs that should already have

A4 Grandfather Rights. If A4 is in that specific area, they are the exact market that you need to pursue.

- Once you have the information, you can use it to write directly to the owner of the HMO and ask if they would be prepared to sell the property or rent the property to you for a fixed period of time. How you use your list will define your success!

Over the past few years, many of my mentees have challenged this strategy, saying things like, "Surely that won't work because everyone is doing it." Well, ask yourself the question of: why is everyone else doing it?

It does work, but only if you take action. Having all the information but taking no action will lead to certain failure. Pick your area carefully by following the due diligence steps I mentioned earlier.

Let's look at building your first marketing campaign by using a "direct to vendor letter." This is a simple letter that you will send to the owner of the HMO from your list. Your letter should be short and direct without offering too many options as this will confuse the recipient.

**Example letter**

Dear Mr./Mrs. Smith,

Please allow me to introduce myself, my name is {insert your name here} and I'm a local property investor based in {insert your area here}. My company specialises in HMOs and management of HMOs.

We are currently interested in acquiring HMO properties in the area of {insert your area here} with a minimum of three bedrooms and two communal rooms. I noticed that you have a similar property situated along {123 Acacia Avenue}.

If you would like to arrange a meeting to see how we may be able to help you turn your HMO into a total hands-off passive investment with a guaranteed rent paid to you each month, or if you would consider selling your property to us, then please feel free to get in touch on the below number.

Kind regards
{Insert your name here}

You can see here that the letter is not complicated and it's easy to read and doesn't waffle on. People don't have the time or the patience to read a load of text, so keep it simple.

This letter is the first introduction and is merely a foot in the door. Don't expect to get any sales from the first campaign. It can take anything from seven to ten campaigns before you start to see results. Tenacity and persistence are the keys to any marketing campaign.

I'm going to share my secret recipe to a successful marketing campaign, so get a pen and be sure to follow the instructions carefully as it's quite a complicated procedure.

**Step 1**. Choose your area (following the Due Diligence)

**Step 2**. Obtain the Licensed HMO Landlord List from your council.

**Step 3**. Draft your letter

**Step 4.** Post your letter

THAT'S IT!!

Don't overcomplicate it, just take action and get the letter out there. You may or may not get a response from your very first campaign and we will go through some sales statistics in a while, but this is just an introduction letter to start things moving and it's all about taking action.

Is building a successful property portfolio as simple as the above steps? No, of course not. But your first marketing campaign really is that simple. Nike has nailed this with their marketing and they state, "just do it!"

To obtain the best results, I recommend you split your HMO Landlord list into three areas. That way you will have one active campaign running all the time without overkilling each area. Here's how I do this.

- Area 1 campaign completed: wait four weeks
- Area 2 campaign begins: wait four weeks
- Area 3 campaign begins wait: four weeks
- Area 1 letter number 2 campaign begins: wait four weeks
- Area 2 letter number 2 campaign begins: wait four weeks
- Area 3 letter number 2 campaign begins: wait four weeks
- Area 1 letter number 3 campaign begins, and so on. You get the point…

Letter number two will be a slightly different format. Make sure you change these for each campaign and keep them simple.

Using this strategy, you will always have an active campaign out at any one time. The more nets that you have cast in the water, the more fish you will catch! Clichéd? Yes, but very true.

Don't worry about using fancy-coloured envelopes either, or wondering if you should handwrite the letters or if you should use first or second-class stamps. In my experience, it doesn't matter. Just get the campaigns out there and stick to the plan.

Remember, at this point, you should already have some form of call answering service in place as discussed earlier in the company structure section.

Now you have your first active campaign, it's going to be a good idea to get some pre-planned questions in place for when you begin to receive calls. I remember receiving my first call. Picture the scene here, I had a lead from our call answering service and the vendor was requesting that I call them back as soon as possible because they needed to move fast. I was thinking 'SHIT, what do I say? I have no idea what to ask. What if they don't take me seriously? What if they think I'm not professional or experienced enough?' What if I get my tongue in a twist and my words don't come out right? My "what ifs" were endless, and I'm positive that you are likely to go through the same emotions if you haven't already! To help you with this, I have included some easy-to-ask questions for you. Please feel free to use these as examples; add to them or take away as you wish.

Vendor telephone questionnaire:

**SMILE** (This will come across in your conversation)

- Ask for their name and write it down.
- Double-check their telephone number and write it down.
- What type of property do they own? i.e. Bungalow, detached etc.
- What type of construction is the property?
- What is the full address and postcode of the property?
- Is the property freehold or leasehold?
- How many bedrooms does the property have?
- How many reception rooms does the property have?
- Who currently lives at the property?
- When was the property purchased?
- Have they done any work on the property? If so, what?
- What is the property worth?
- Has it been valued? If so, when and by whom?
- Ask about the situation. Are they looking to sell quickly?
- Is the property on the market? If so, how long for and who with?
- What is the timescale in which they would like to sell?
- Is there a mortgage on the property?
- Are there any arrears attached to the property?
- Are there any early redemption fees?

Once you have this information, you can then begin your due diligence on the property. My advice is to keep in touch with the vendor and make sure the lead doesn't go cold.

After three to four weeks, you should begin your next campaign targeting area number two using the same letter and follow the same format. The next step is to wait until the calls come flooding in. Don't expect this from your very first campaign though, as it will take time as per the statistics shown below.

Research has proved that tenacity is the key when it comes to sales. Apparently, around 50% of people never bother to follow up on a sale... whereas 80% of sales are made on the fifth to the twelfth contact!

You therefore need to be consistent and proactive with your sales campaign, as doing nothing will not bring any rewards. I couldn't believe it when I first saw this information.

It proves that tenacity is the key here. Don't give up on the first, or second campaign, as it's unlikely you will get any deals at this stage. As you can see though, the more consistent you are, the more successful you are likely to be. I have a copy of these statistics on my office wall just to remind my staff not to quit!

**Leaflet campaigns**

**Do leaflets work?**

Yes, if done correctly, that's why we have dozens of them each week landing on our doormat! Here are a few things to consider with leaflets:

Target your area well by postcode and make sure that the area will suit your chosen tenant demographic. For example, don't leaflet a rural area with no transport links.

Make sure the leaflet is brightly-coloured, precise, and to the point with no waffle and keep the sentences short and easy to understand. For example:

"Are you a landlord?

Are you looking for a hassle-free guaranteed rent for your property regardless of tenant voids?

If so call now on 012-3456 to arrange a confidential chat."

Add some nice pictures of your company logo (get a logo); this is just an example for you to build upon. Each leaflet campaign should be targeting around 6,000 houses, so think big! As always, don't give up after your first campaign. Go back to the sales statistics chart on the previous page and be consistent.

I know lots of investors that have tried to deliver the leaflets themselves to save money; please don't be like them. Don't deliver the leaflets yourself. There are plenty of leaflet franchise companies out there. Just Google them and choose the one that suits you.

**TIP:** Don't go cheap and have them delivered inside a newspaper, as the chances are they will end up in the bin.

### Online Web Portals

There are many online web portals that can help you source property, so let's look first at Rightmove.co.uk

The average number of properties listed on Rightmove is 800,000, so this makes Rightmove the Daddy of property search websites. It's the best place to compare houses on the market, as well as boasting an amazing number of properties up for grabs. If you are time short, then Rightmove allows you to set up email alerts to make finding properties even easier.

**Tip**: Set up alerts across all of the web property portals, but be very specific. For example, set up alerts in areas for four-bed houses at £X and then another alert for three-bed houses at £X so when the email comes through it is really quick to assess if the property is right for you.

**Tip**: Use the 'Contact All' facility on the portal, you can search an area or a city and then you can select to 'Contact All' estate agents that have those results in your town. Don't expect too much from this tactic, but it is much leveraged and time efficient.

Expect a low response from agents though as sometimes they just won't bother calling you back.

I wonder where they fit into the sales statistic chart. The more specific you are with your requirements, the better chance you have of being taken seriously, and may begin to receive responses.

The follow-up is important, repeat this exercise a week later and refer to the fact that you contacted them last week, but heard nothing.

# Zoopla.co.uk

Zoopla advertises an average of 500,000 properties, and it's another big search engine. In some areas it's the number one for estate agents to advertise on; it also has a great keywords search facility.

> **Tip**: Zoopla is great for spotting lease purchase options, and you can quickly see if the house is in negative equity or close to the last sale price. The last purchase price is displayed on Zoopla dating back to 1995 and the floor plans are also easily accessed.

> **Tip**: Use the keywords analysis to find motivated sellers by putting in the search 'no chain' or 'some modernisation required' or 'in need of some updating' etc.

> **Tip**: Use the keywords 'separate units' or similar 'separate flats' to find title split deals.

> **Tip**: Use keywords 'motivated vendor'. You will be surprised by how many estate agents use this language.

# Mouseprice.com

Mouseprice is one of my favourite property platforms and has great ways of listing properties that have been on the market before and haven't sold. We purchased our very first HMO property because of the analysis that Mouseprice offered. We were able to see the property had been on and off the market for about three years and had failed to sell. When we eventually viewed the property, sure enough, the vendor was very motivated and did need to sell quickly. And at a discount, as I mentioned earlier.

## Walk the estate agents' strip

If your town is anything like ours, 80% of the estate agents are located in about two streets, so start making yourself known! Go and see them. You can make yourself memorable by taking in a cake or a biscuit tin (tape a business card to the top)

Forming relationships is very important and you want to be in the position to be able to have a catch-up with an agent and find out what they might have coming on the market.

Think win-win. If an agent can tell a potential vendor they may have someone interested in their house before they even go to market, they will certainly put you at the top of their contact list for the next deal!

Diarise to catch up with estate agents on a regular basis and if you can, obtain the agent's email address. Remember a lot of them are out of the office most days. Pop them an email every week; remember that consistency is the key. Wait any longer than a week and they may have forgotten you.

Ask them: have they valued any houses this week? Is there anything coming on the market that you might be interested in? And don't be afraid to say, "Me again. Just reminding you I'm still here and still looking for something. No need to reply. I just wanted to keep you updated."

## Local newspapers

Many newspapers often have adverts from buyers offering to buy houses for cash and fast; you may have seen the adverts. In fact, they are similar to the leaflet campaigns that we run ourselves.

You are trying to find motivated vendors. If you see a few of these adverts in your local paper, it may mean this strategy works well in that area for attracting motivated sellers. If you choose to advertise in papers, the longer you commit to advertising the cheaper the cost. Personally, I have had very limited results in newspaper advertising.

## Networking

Love it or hate it, networking is very often a good place to tell strangers what you do, and it's extremely powerful.

You will find many property events around the country. Some are free and some you may need to pay a few pounds to join. Either way, use the group to its full advantage.

Networking for some can be a daunting thought. I know it used to be for me until I realised how amazingly powerful it was.

Through our network, we raised all of the finances we needed in the first year to fund every HMO. Over the next few years, we went on to buy million pound properties with partners we met through our network.

Even if you struggle, or if you're not a people person, it's important that you stretch yourself out of your comfort zone and get yourself out there. If you don't network, then how will people know who you are or what it is that you are looking for?

Go armed with business cards and tell people how you can help them with their property problems.

There are lots of property networking events up and down the country, most of which will allow you around twenty seconds of "pitch time", so make sure that you take full advantage of this. You might not be in the same room with these people ever again. This is your opportunity to tell people what you do and how you can help them.

> **TIP:** Write a twenty-second pitch. Make it precise and to the point. Practise it and be sure to use it at EVERY networking event you go to. If you attend with your partner, then have two separate pitches and sit separately from each other.

Here is my pitch; feel free to use this as a starting point:

*"Hi, my name is Rick Gannon and I'm a local investor based in Worcester.*

*I specialise in HMOs and have hundreds of rooms within the area.*

*If you are interested in HMOs or if you think I may be able to help you with your HMO issue or problem, then please find me during the break."*

Don't get too caught up with this. It really is just an icebreaker to tell people why you are there.

You won't have time at the networking event to have a full meeting with anyone, but others will know why you are there and you can exchange business cards and arrange a coffee at a later date.

Get yourself booked on to the next property networking event in your area.

A great compliment to this would be joining a valued Facebook Property Group and begin to network online. It's not quite as powerful, but it's a start.

Most Facebook groups won't allow advertising, so be respectful of their rules. I run a successful Facebook group called 'The HMO Community Group' so make sure you join today and be sure to say 'Hi' by introducing yourself.

**House clearance businesses**

Here's a totally off-the-wall suggestion!

House clearance companies are, by the pure nature of their business, going to be attending lots of vacant properties every week; some may be deceased estates, some may be from divorcing couples and so on.

Why not offer to advertise your company on their vans and as a reward make a monthly contribution to their business as a sponsor? This way, your name will be seen by any person that has an involvement with the house. It is very targeted marketing, but nobody ever seems to do it. Why? Because most people don't think outside the box! That's what makes the serious investors stand out from the rest.

## Interview marketing campaign

This is a very different and innovative way to position yourself as the local property expert and is deliberately made to look like a magazine or a newspaper article.

Commission someone to write a magazine-style article about you and your business. You know the type, like a Q&A interview with lots of questions about you and your business. You can write this yourself if you really want to, even on a Word document. (Don't forget to include your contact details)

Once you have written it, you can contact your local trade magazine, (we all have one) the trade magazines that local businesses advertise in, you know the type.

Request to advertise in there for one month and send the interview off to them to publish. It will cost less than £100 and when it's published, they should send you a copy too.

When you receive your copy, it appears that you have been interviewed by a local magazine about your property company. Photocopy the interview, and send it to everyone on your landlord register with a sticky note, saying something like, "Hi John (take the name from the register), I saw this and thought they might be able to help you." Sign it with a "J," put the article into an envelope and handwrite the name and address of the landlord that you have taken from your landlord list.

When it's received by the recipient, it looks like one of their associates has read about you and your property company in a magazine and has torn out the page, or photocopied it and sent it directly to them with a sticky note on. It doesn't look like a regular letter and doesn't appear to have come from you!

We will then follow this up, about two to three weeks later, with a normal marketing campaign sent from us which cements our brand with the recipient. Now that's a new way of marketing! Give it a try and see what results you get back. You may be very surprised. This campaign is probably only going to work once so make sure you are on the ball and the article looks professional.

## What do you do when the phone starts ringing?

When potential clients start to respond to your campaign, the calls should (if you have followed the steps listed so far) be directed to your call answering service, and you will be notified by email and text with all the necessary details you need to call the client back.

Be prepared. By this I mean be in the right environment when you call them back; in a nice quiet room free from noise and distraction. Research the property on Google street view prior to the conversation so that you can picture it in your mind. Have your call sheet ready and rehearse the questions beforehand. More importantly, don't panic – and be yourself. People mainly buy from people so be happy, friendly and polite. Don't forget to smile even though you are on the phone as this will come across in your conversation.

If you are asked a question that you can't answer, then don't lie. Always be honest with them and tell them you don't know, but you will find out and call them back. Honesty and transparency are the only ways that we should operate as professionals and we should always work to that rule.

That's all you need to do at this stage. Now, you have all the information you need to begin your due diligence and marketing.

## Motivated sellers

Ideally, we only want to purchase property below market value, which should be at the 25% mark. Most mortgage providers will offer a 75% loan to value product on an HMO. If we can source them at a 25% discount and, if we then refurbish the property, and show that we have improved it, we may be able to refinance the property later at the uplifted value and recycle our deposit money out. We can then use the same formula to buy our next house and so on.

This should mean that the house didn't cost you anything to buy. You may need to refurbish the property though.

Why would anyone sell their property below market value? That is a common question, and, in my experience, a seller's motivation may change on a daily basis. It could be that they are:

- Going through a divorce and need to sell quickly.
- Moving abroad and need to sell quickly.
- It may be a deceased estate and several people are involved.
- It could be a bank repossession.
- The property may have been on the market for a while and they just want their money out.
- There may be problems with the property that need remedying.
- They may need to raise cash to help a relative.
- And many more reasons.

Be careful, because it can become very easy to become a motivated buyer! Buying at the wrong price could tie up all your cash, resulting in you running out of deposits pretty quickly.

## Viewing the property

After speaking with the prospective client/vendor, you will need to conduct your due diligence to ensure that the property will work for you as an HMO. Before you decide to view it, here are the first things that you need to consider.

Is the property already an HMO?

This will depend on which campaign you attracted the lead from. If the lead has come from your HMO landlord list, then it is likely it will already be an HMO.

If the property isn't already an HMO, then you need to check to see if Article 4 Planning Direction is in place in that area as this may prevent you changing the use of the property. (You should already have done this when choosing your target area.)

The next step is to make an appointment with the vendor and view the property.

A few points to note here: you are looking to see if the property will be suitable, but you are also using this meeting to forge a relationship with the seller.

Remember that people buy from people, and if you are polite and friendly from the outset, this will show that you are a professional.

Always smile and be friendly. I know lots of professional investors that go out of their way in order to insult the property and say things like, "Oh, whoever chose those carpets?" and "Wow! What a really old-fashioned kitchen."

Don't do this. It's rude and will put the seller straight off you.

Remember, if the person showing you the house is the owner, they may have been in a similar position as you are now when they began their journey and they would have put a lot of time and effort into the house at some point. Regardless of how tired the property looks, remain impartial and professional.

Get to know the seller, find out what it is that makes them tick. Ask them why they are selling and try to understand what their pain is. If we can understand this, then we may be able to help them.

We are looking to see if the area is suitable, what the condition of the property is, are the sizes of the rooms compliant with the licensing standards for your area, or will the property need to be altered to facilitate this?

Does the property have sufficient bathrooms and toilets to satisfy the required regulations, or would it need en-suites or extra bathrooms fitted?

Never make an offer at the viewing. Explain to the vendor that you will go away and conduct some research and you will be back in touch with them in a few days.

## Valuing the property

Valuing a property as a potential HMO is a skillset in itself, but there are lots of tools out there to help you with this.

Here are some of the tools I use every day to help me:

Search www.rightmove.co.uk and see if there are any local comparable properties in the area that have sold recently.

Search www.zoopla.co.uk and do the same.

Search www.mouseprice.com and do the same.

Call a local agent and ask their opinion, based on their knowledge.

If you are still not confident, you can (if you are prepared to pay) instruct a RICS valuation (Registered Institute of Chartered Surveyors) who will give you a full report and a valuation. This way you have a professional valuation from a qualified surveyor; this is a good option as mortgage providers will use a similar process. All these tools will give you an informed decision on how much the property maybe worth.

There are some misconceptions in the property industry on how to value an HMO. Please don't be misled by thinking that all converted property will be revalued by up to ten times the gross rent! This is a misconception, and although it can be possible, provided the property meets certain criteria, such as significant fundamental changes to the property which no longer renders it as a true house. If the house is licensed and in A4 area, then it may be possible to obtain a commercial valuation if it is already a commercial property such as a converted pub or converted office block.

In my experience, if it looks like a house and it smells like a house, then the likelihood is that it will be valued as a house. Use this as a benchmark and you won't be disappointed.

Don't be taken in by vendors and agents who may value a three-bedroom house as a five-bedroom house because they have simply put a bed in the living room and a bed in the dining room! It's still a three-bedroom house!

## Making an offer

You have, by now, conducted your due diligence in terms of the area, A4 Planning, licensing, stacking the deal, and room sizes. Let's quickly revisit this anyway because I want you to be completely sure.

This example is a purchase of a six-bedroom, already licensed HMO:

- Agreed purchase price £200,000
- Deposit required 25% = £50,000
- Stamp duty £7,500
- Refurbishment £10,000 (already converted)
- Solicitors fees £1,000
- Total money required £68,500

Six bedrooms achieving £400 each = £2,400
Minus 10% for voids = £240.00
Minus 5% maintenance = £120.00
Cleaning costs £60 per month
Insurance £40 per month

Misc. £50 per month
Mortgage-based on 6% interest only
(we always use 6% which allows for increase's in rates)
= £750 pcm

Monthly net cash flow = £1,140
ROI = annual profit = £13,680
Divided by Initial investment £68,500
X 100

**ROI 19.9%**

Is this a good deal for you? It would be if the property was actually worth £274,000, then you know it will be a no money left in the deal when you refinance at 75% loan to value which means that the ROI is infinite. Sound good?

Once you have conducted all the due diligence, and, if the deal meets your criteria, it's time to make that offer! Don't forget that you should know what the house is worth. You should be looking to recycle your deposit money and refurb money back. This doesn't necessarily mean that you have to make a ridiculous offer as this is likely to put the vendor off and it may insult them, resulting in you losing the deal altogether. There are many ways of gaining the deposit back out. As I mentioned before, one of which is by adding value by refurbishment and or adding rooms to the house.

Now you are comfortable with your figures. You know that the property is, or will be, suitable. You are happy that the property has or will have the correct planning permission. You are happy that the room sizes will be suitable. You are happy with the monthly cash flow and the return on investment and you are happy that you have sufficient funds (or will have) in order to go ahead with the purchase. (Always speak with a mortgage advisor to find out your current position.) Now give the vendor or the agent a call and make your offer. I always follow this through with a polite email which affirms everything.

Wait to see what their reaction is. I would leave it for a few days, and if I hadn't heard anything, then I would chase them up with a polite phone call.

If the vendor is happy to proceed at this point, you should agree the terms in writing (Heads of Terms) and send them to the vendor for them to populate the details of their chosen solicitor. If you are working with an agent, then they will usually do this for you in a memorandum of sale. This document would then be sent to your solicitor to begin the contracts of the sale and the searches.

If the vendor rejects your offer, that doesn't mean they may not be interested in doing a deal in the future. Make sure you have a follow-up system where you can log all your leads and your deals, i.e. something you can refer back to at a later stage.

We constantly get deals from our follow-up box. The last one being a £1.1 million-pound block of flats that we couldn't agree on at the time, but two years later, we made the purchase after a series of follow up calls.

You now have an idea of the process and you will need to begin your next campaign shortly, so you will need to design a new letter!

Here is an example of our second letter campaign:

New Era Property Solutions Ltd
XXXXXXX
XXXXX
Office;
Mobile;
«Mr_McDermott»
X House
«Area»
«Postcode»
Dear X,

I wrote to you a few months ago looking to see if there was a way I could help you with your HMO properties.

I wanted to update you on some of the ways we have helped other landlords in Worcester recently. If you have an empty property or want to release the equity in your house, the following options might be for you:

**1. Existing HMOs Purchased – Benefits to you, the Landlord**

- Certainty of sale to you. We understand what's involved in running an HMO.
- Speed of transaction, we can exchange and complete in a few weeks.
- Existing tenants can transfer with the property, no need to terminate anyone's tenancy (subject to terms).
- No refurbishments required. We are taking all properties in any condition.

## 2. Guaranteed Rental Of Property From You To Me, Landlord to Landlord – Benefits to you the Landlord

- We can guarantee fixed rental of HMOs for three years giving you certainty. No letting agents, no tenants, no ASTs to manage. Hassle free! Guaranteed rent whether occupied or not.
- Guaranteed maintenance.
- Peace of mind that you are renting your HMO to someone who understands the workings of an HMO. You'll be able to go away on holiday, worry free!
- Refurbish your property, no cost to you.
- Provide furniture and new beds to the landlord's property, no further outlay from you.
- The house maintains an HMO status which is potentially more valuable than converting to a single let, where HMO status can be lost. Your asset is still working hard for you.
- The property is now providing an income back to you, no voids or empty properties to worry about.
- You are covering your costs and also accruing the equity for the future.

If you are interested in any of the above, we would be happy to discuss this in person or over the phone, so please feel free to get in touch. We can offer a quick decision, without the need for you to pay any agent's fees. We hope to hear from you soon.

Yours Sincerely,
Mr/Mrs X
Office; 000111333 Mobile; 07XXXXXXXX

As you can see this is a very different letter than the first campaign. Feel free to use this as a template for your own.

By now we had two HMOs, both of which were fully occupied. We were on our second marketing campaign, and our call answering service was taking calls from our campaigns on a daily basis. Our list of leads was growing, and I could see the future of the business was looking rosy.

I had a list of properties that I needed to view and dealt with them on a first-come, first-served basis as I was only targeting the area that I lived in. I knew the streets pretty well and was able to dismiss the properties that I thought weren't suitable quickly.

> **TIP**: Get an easy to use spreadsheet ready so you can quickly stack deals as they come in. This way you don't need to spend unnecessary time on leads that won't work for you.

> **TIP:** Have an easy-to-use follow-up system that you can place any junk leads in and revisit them every few months. We use a Customer/Client Relationship Manager (CRM) called Less Annoying CRM. It tracks leads and allows you to update them easily.

Be prepared to say no. Remember that not every lead will fit within your criteria; don't get bogged down wasting time on viewing houses that don't work for you.

If it doesn't work, then park it and place it into your follow-up box.

# Chapter 9
# Working with Partners and Investors

I had secured a meeting with a nice, friendly man who responded to our second campaign. He lived in London but invested in property all over the country. He had a property close to our new HMOs, so we arranged an appointment to meet each other at 10am that Wednesday.

As always, I was prompt and arrived at 9:30am. The man I was meeting was already there and standing outside waiting for me. The property was massive and situated bang in the middle of Studentville. It looked a little tired on the outside and wasn't much better on the inside either. It had bare floors and the whole house was covered, top to toe, in woodchip wallpaper that had been painted with white gloss. It really was a mess!

The seller's motivation was that the property had failed to let for the next student year (owing to the state of the décor, I presume) and the agent had let him down on several occasions with false promises.

Despite all of this, the property had great potential and was in the right area. The owner wasn't keen on anything but a straight sale, but after several negotiations and meetings later, we agreed on an exchange of contracts at the price of £300,000, to be completed in five years' time. In the meantime, I would lease the property from him and trade it as an HMO (exchange with a delayed completion).

The vendor explained that he had no equity in the property, and he had attempted to sell it on several occasions for £280,000, but had failed. He was quite happy to wait five years for the extra £20,000, which meant that he would come out with a profit at the end of the deal.

Everything was looking good and we agreed to put down a deposit of £10,000 upon exchange of contracts, so he had something to show for it upfront. This was to be deducted from the asking price at the point of completion.

The property had eight bedrooms, all of which would have achieved £400 each. None were en-suite and the property needed at least £30,000 spending on it. Therefore, the total investment was around £40,000. There was also a contingency of £10,000 for unforeseen works and legal costs and contracts which meant we were looking for around £50,000 in order to complete the deal.

Although our cashflow had begun to improve with our newly-founded HMOs, we still had little available money. However, this deal was too good to miss, as it would bring a £1,200 a month profit. I also valued the property at around £350,000 in five years' time, based on a bricks and mortar valuation.

Be aware if using this strategy, as you are committed to the purchase. Once you exchange the contracts, stamp duty will be payable upon the signing of the legal documents (upon exchange). This means you will need to plan ahead to ensure you have the funds in place to complete the purchase when the time arises.

I immediately went to my network, which at the time was a small group of investors that met each month to discuss property. I put the deal on the table. Within a few hours, I had an offer for all of the money, based on a 50/50 split of the profits and 50% of the equity of the property.

This was music to my ears and affirms that you don't need your own money to invest in property. If you find a truly good deal, you will always find the money, provided you are fair with the partnership and you are open and honest at all times. Win-win situation.

The investor was a genuinely nice chap and had wanted to invest in HMOs for some time, but owing to time spent away with his full-time job, he didn't have the time, nor the experience. Before discussing the deal with him, we agreed to refer him to a financial advisor to take independent advice. This is now a requirement under the Financial Control Act and is a safeguard for both parties. Once independent financial advice is undertaken then the investor/partner can be certified as either a "High Net Worth Individual" or as a "Sophisticated Investor". Once this has taken place, you are free to go ahead and do the deal together.

This process is put in place to safeguard both parties and to prove that any investor or partner is clear on the deal as well as any risk involved. It also shows that they were in the right frame of mind and hadn't been pressured into the deal. If the deal structure collapses in the future resulting in any litigation, then you can prove that the partner had taken independent advice at that time.

We had several meetings at the prospective HMO and also at my house. My future joint venture partner had been certified by our IFA as a High Net Worth Individual, and we were happy with the structure in principle. After conducting due diligence on each other, we decided all was good and agreed to do the deal together using his funds.

The offer was put forward to the vendor and duly accepted. Heads of Terms were submitted and forwarded to relevant solicitors. It was time for a holiday!

Off we went to Tenerife for two weeks in the sun (again). Everything was in place with the big deal, and there was nothing I could do, so it was decided it was time for a break.

We were about four to five weeks into the deal at this point, and solicitors were busying away writing contracts. I was at the pool bar with my family sipping on an ice cold mojito in the blistering sunshine, when I went back to my sun bed. I stupidly checked my emails on my phone and saw a long message from my newly-acquired joint venture partner explaining that he had thought long and hard about our deal and felt that the risk level was too high. He no longer wanted to go ahead and was subsequently pulling out!

I was a little perplexed, as we had both put a lot of time into this, but he made his position clear that he felt it was too risky and he was out.

Great! I'm away from the UK and now I don't have any cash to complete on this big deal. However, being the positive person that I am, it didn't worry me too much. I knew that it was a good deal and I would be sure to find the money.

I immediately emailed my solicitor and explained that I would now be going alone on this and to amend the contracts into my own name.

Fourteen days flew by, and our holiday was over. We returned to the UK, and a day later, straight back to work. My first appointment was to meet the vendor back at the property, so I could measure up and start pricing the refurb. Fortunately, I didn't have to explain that my partner had pulled out as he didn't know the management structure. Also, I had already secured another investor. This time, on a loan-only basis for a fixed return, which meant that I got to keep the whole of the property and the cash flow. Result!

As I arrived at the property, sure enough, the vendor was already there, but he seemed a little quiet and didn't want to chat too much. He was quite unresponsive to my questions and non-committal when I asked questions on timelines for exchange. I didn't let this put me off. Ever the optimist, I put it down to him having a bad day. I took my measurements, thanked him and left, and that was the last I saw him. In fact, it was the last time I ever spoke to him!

Several weeks passed, and my solicitor was badgering me for a completion date. I had attempted on several occasions to contact the vendor, but heard nothing. He simply wouldn't return my calls.

Out of the blue, I received an email from him apologising that he hadn't got back to me but there had been a terrible accident and he had lost two members of his close family in a car accident and had been pre-occupied. That was the last contact we had. From that point on he didn't reply to any correspondence either from my solicitor or from me and the deal fell through costing me several hundreds of pounds for aborted fees! I firmly believe it was never meant to be and quickly realised that every deal was vulnerable to failing at any time, but that's property, and that's business!

> **TIP:** Be prepared to pay for aborted fees. It's a business cost that sometimes can't be avoided. Always have a backup investor in place where possible should the primary investor decide not to go through with the deal.

Working with partners and investors is mainly about building relationships. It's absolutely not just about raising cash and leveraging skills/assets.

There are many things you will need to consider when working with a partner or an investor. Firstly, this is more about the relationship you have with each other than anything else. Ask yourself the following questions when deciding on any potential partnership:

What synergy do you have with each other? I mean how long have you known each other? Do you know each other really well and are you happy that you can work together or have you only just met? If it's the latter, then you will need to forge your relationship before entering into business together. This can take months, even years, before you may be comfortable.

Are your values aligned? Are you looking to achieve similar goals? What are your goals? Are you both looking to grow a great property portfolio to achieve financial freedom? How well do you know each other? Did you meet at a networking meeting yesterday or have you known each other for years? What skills are you both bringing to the table? What is it about this partnership that would work? It can't just be about the money.

Do you have anything in writing? You may have known each other for one year or even ten or more years. Regardless of this, you need to make sure that you write down any agreement you have with each other.

Sometimes things get forgotten over time, and what you thought you had agreed upon at the last coffee meeting may have been distorted or forgotten. Make sure, whatever you agree to, is written down in the form of a contract or a partnership agreement and minute every meeting.

I would advise that the partnership document is commissioned by a solicitor or an accountant rather than doing it yourself. If you do choose to do it yourself, it's still better than not having anything in place at all.

- Be sure to conduct your due diligence. If you are going into business with someone that is not a family member, and someone that you haven't known for years, then you will be required under the FCA regulations to have this person certified by an independent financial advisor as either a sophisticated investor or a High Net Worth Individual.

This isn't a complicated procedure and your IFA can guide you through this. It has been put into place to protect both parties should the partnership go wrong, and to prevent the partner attempting to sue you, stating that they were not fully aware of the deal at the time.

Here are a few DD tips when working with partners.

- Request your partner's current credit file (don't expect to keep this, but you will at least need to read it).
- Request a copy of two utility bills to prove their address and take a copy of their passport.
- If they already have property, then ask to see the title deeds.
- If they have a limited company, then check their accounts on Company's House or on the internet.
- Be fully prepared to offer the same courtesy back.

Working with a partner or an investor can be an extremely enjoyable and fruitful experience. It may accelerate your success, if done correctly. Equally, it can also be a painful and miserable experience should the partnership crumble. So please do your due diligence, and only enter into a partnership if you are 100% in alignment with each other.

# Chapter 10
# Tenants and House Information

T he phone continued to ring with leads, and the next stop was to view a property lead that had come from our second campaign.

It was a great house; mid-terrace with two converted attic rooms (no dormers just Velux windows), three bedrooms on the middle floor, and a converted dining room (bedroom) downstairs with a great communal room and a separate kitchen.

This was already an HMO with a five-year licence for six people. I met the vendor at the house and he explained to me that he had purchased the property along with his wife in 2006 (close to the peak of the market) as an investment and a pension fund for the future. The housing market then crashed and they were instantly placed into negative equity. They initially began to manage the property themselves, but having no experience as landlords, they decided it wasn't for them and decided to rent it to a local charity for children and young adults.

The vendor had nothing but bad things to say about the house. Since they rented it to the charity, they had only had complaints from neighbours about the anti-social behaviour being caused in the property and regular calls from the police stating that they needed to gain entry. They decided that letting the house to the charity wasn't the way forward for them, and subsequently, gave them notice to leave.

It was now empty and costing them several hundred pounds each month in mortgage payments. They had simply had enough and were very motivated to off-load the house at this point.

To begin with, they were only interested in selling the house as they wanted to clear their debt with the bank and put it down to experience and walk away. The problem was that they had the house valued by a local agent and (in my opinion) it was overvalued by around £20,000 at that time and they were asking for £220,000. The best I could get to was £190,000 based on local comparisons.

They couldn't accept this, as they owed the bank more as they were in negative equity. The house itself didn't need a great deal doing to it and was in relatively good order. It was in a private block of terraced houses with a small car parking space and it fitted well within my criteria.

After the viewing, I went away and conducted all the necessary due diligence and worked out that I could potentially purchase the property at the asking price of £220,000 in five years on a lease purchase option. In the meantime, I could pay the owner around £750 a month based on the single-let value for a house of this size in this area; this way I would also make around £800 a month profit.

I called the vendor and explained the detail to him. I made sure I got the point across, without being disrespectful, that I believed the property was overvalued in the current market. This way he got to clear the bank's debt and walk away with a few thousand pounds on top; also, he would be making money each month from the rent. He was very interested and said in principle that we might have a deal, but he would need to discuss it with his wife.

He got back to me a day later with a resounding 'no'. He felt that the property market would increase dramatically over the next five years and the house would potentially be worth much more than £220,000.

While talking this through on the phone, I immediately revised my offer. This time, offering the same £220,000 for the house in five years, but with 25% of any uplift over and above that price, should the house increase in value. He was instantly impressed and said, again, that this would be agreeable in principle, but he would have to ask his wife and again, and he would get back to me. I also felt that this was a great deal as it offered more security for him, and likewise, I was confident that the market would grow in order to sustain the extra 25% while also offering a great yield for me too.

The vendor returned my call a day later with yet again a resounding 'no'. He explained that his wife wasn't happy with the offer, as she was very sure that the growth of the equity over five years would be considerably more.

I once again re-adjusted my offer and, this time, I suggested the same deal, only with offering them 50% of any growth above the agreed price but, you guessed it, this was also rejected. The vendor stated that they had decided they just wanted to walk away with a straightforward sale.

I wished them all the best and we ended the conversation. The deal was placed in our follow-up box alongside many others that didn't fit within our criteria at that time.

We continued with our marketing campaign and the leads were falling in thick and fast with many landlords wanting to sell, but all seemed to have delusions of grandeur with the prices. After explaining to them that we were not in any position to be able to offer such prices, many of them agreed that we could take the property on a lease or management agreement over a period of three to five years with a guaranteed rent paid to them regardless of voids.

The phone rang. It was my personal mobile and it was a number I instantly recognised. The vendor from last month that had turned down my offers of a lease option. "Hi Rick, I was wondering if you were still interested in the property as we still haven't had any offers." Mmmm, let me think about that.

We eventually agreed on the deal and secured it on a rent-to-rent contract. The vendor was adamant that they wouldn't lock in a price for a lease purchase, but they didn't want the burden of running the property and it was currently empty and costing them money.

We verbally agreed to take the property over on a rent-to-rent management agreement for a three-year period, and to pay them £750 a month, which we guaranteed even if the property was vacant. We were also responsible for paying all the utility bills and for the maintenance and repair of the property (excluding the main building and excluding the central heating system). We instructed our solicitors and the deal was completed about fourteen days later. Within three weeks, we had decorated the whole house, and every room had been reserved with working professional tenants!

## Rent-to-Rent

A rent-to-rent agreement is where you take over the management of the property under a legally binding management agreement between you or your company and the owner of the property. During the term, which would typically be between three to five years, you would normally be responsible for the maintenance and the decoration of the interior of the property. You would also be responsible for the sourcing and the management of the tenants including the collection of the rent.

Typically, you would offer a guaranteed rent, which you would pay to the owner each month, regardless of the property being tenanted or not. You would be responsible for any payment of council tax and all the utility bills.

Things to consider with the Rent-to-Rent strategy

- The owner of the house will need the correct mortgage product for an HMO with the necessary consent-to-let given by the provider.
- The owner of the property should be responsible for providing their own buildings insurance declaring that it's an HMO and listing you as an interested party.
- The owner would retain responsibility for any repairs to the roof and the windows.
- The owner would retain responsibility for repairs to the gas boiler (but not the periodic annual checks as that usually lies with you).

- The owner would usually retain responsibility for the fire alarm system (but not the routine periodic checks as that would lie with you).
- Responsibility for periodic checks of the electrical installation can be negotiated, but we usually take that responsibility too.
- All other responsibilities would usually rest with you.
- As it's a contract between you and the owner, you can change any of the above as you wish, as long as it's a win for both parties.
- Always have your contracts drawn up by a property specialist solicitor. There are lots of Rent-to-Rent agreements flying around the internet as most people like to help others where possible. You can source agreements for free if you know where to look. My advice is never to do this! Every deal is different and every person's tax situation is unique to them. If you are serious about setting up a sustainable business, then be prepared to spend a few pounds and have your agreement commissioned by a professional and tailored to your individual needs. You may never have to refer back to the agreement and I truly hope that you don't, but it's there to safeguard both you and the owner.
- I am constantly asked by students in my mentoring programme to share my legal documents, but I'm afraid it's always the same answer. After all, they pay me for sound advice!
- The other thing to consider is VAT. Will your new Rent-to-Rent company be expected to pay it? Don't forget that we don't charge VAT on rent, but if you are offering a service on a Rent-to-Rent agreement, then you *may* be liable for paying VAT. Once you have your

agreement written, it's good practice to ask a property specialist Accountant to take a look at them in order to guide you further with this element.

Rent-to-Rent can be a great way of growing your portfolio without having to put large amounts of money down for deposits, but be aware that you don't own the property so you will need to keep costs to a minimum. Ideally, you should look to recoup any start-up cost in the first twelve months.

Remember that you are guaranteeing the rent, and this is a huge commitment, which means that you will be legally obliged to pay this even if the property is empty.

*

By now, the deals were coming in thick and fast and over the following few months, we had acquired around eleven HMOs which were bringing in considerably more than I was earning as a police officer. I was still officially a warranted officer, albeit I wasn't getting paid as I was on a career break. The defining moment when I decided actually to resign came around six months later.

# Chapter 11
# Choosing Tenants

O ur tenants are our customers, and should be treated as such. They will define your business, so it's best to get this correct at the beginning. (we will talk about this later in the systems paragraph). You will need to choose which tenant demographic you would like to cater for in your properties.

## White collar professionals

This is the demographic of tenant that we choose for our business. White collar professionals are people that usually have a formal qualification, and they will work in high-end professions such as doctors, pilots, chemists, and accountants.

I find that this demographic of tenant need with hardly any looking after, and they like to be left alone to enjoy the house. We don't often hear from them.

## Blue collar workers

Likely to be employed in a factory or warehouse, the majority of our blue collar tenants are from Eastern Europe and make for very good tenants. We find them very clean and very hard working.

## Students

Students can be both good and bad at the same time! They will usually stay for ten or eleven months of the year, which is great, as once you check them in they are now in situ for that academic year. Students will almost always come with a guarantor, who will usually be a parent and, if for any reason they miss a month's rent, then all it takes is a quick phone call to Mum or Dad and usually, the rent is in your bank within a few minutes.

## Local Housing Authority

These are usually people that don't have a full-time job, and are supported by the Local Authority, or possibly on disability benefit.

This demographic would mean that they are likely to be in the house most of the time, which means that they will be using more electric, water and gas.

The local council may pay their rent directly to you but beware, if the tenant fails to complete a form correctly, then their payments may be stopped and you may have to wait for your rent.

The choice on tenant demographic is entirely up to you, and the great thing about being the boss is that you can choose.

A few months into my journey, I was sat outside a property waiting for a BT engineer to come and install the Wi-Fi. This wasn't an unusual practice as they often didn't turn up. (Plan this well in advance). When they did, on many occasions, they couldn't install it owing to some crazy unforeseen issue such as they forgot the router or they couldn't connect to the box in the street as every port was in use – even though I had booked this about six weeks in advance. Anyway, there I was, sitting in my car outside the property, when I saw a police van and a police car pull up behind me. I immediately recognised three out of the four officers that got out and, likewise, they also recognised me as it was my old team. Not just the guys from the nick, it was the team that I was posted to, the team that I had risked my life with on many occasions! They saw me immediately and walked over to my car. We started chatting and, to begin with, I thought they had stopped to chat to me as they recognised my car.

After chatting for about two minutes or so, one of the officers said, "Well, we can't stop. We are on a job, we are looking for ..." and he went on to say the address of the property. If I'm completely honest, it just didn't register that they were talking about my newly-acquired lease option that I was sitting directly outside.

They even asked if I knew the person they were looking for and told me his name. Once again it just didn't click. We stopped chatting, and they began running towards the door of the house about to force entry.

"Wait!" I shouted and clambered out of the car over to the house. "I'll let you in! This is my house!"

"Oh, it's your house, is it Rick? Why didn't you say?"

"I didn't realise.  It just didn't twig."

"Mmmm," was the stern reply.

I duly opened the door and let them in. They confirmed the name of the person they were looking for, and now it had sunk in, I sheepishly led them upstairs and to the room of the tenant they were looking for. As they opened the door, just to add to my embarrassment, the tenant was lying on the bed smoking cannabis!

My ex-colleagues now were saying very little to me, and the only interaction was the odd disapproving glare in my direction. They handcuffed the tenant and arrested him for breaching his bail conditions.

A fleeting comment from my ex-colleague as they marched him from the premises, "So this is what you are doing now is it, Rick, harbouring criminals?" Ouch!

Off he went in the back of the police car and I never saw him again!

This tenant was a young man aged around twenty-two. He had a good job at the local highly-acclaimed spa as a chef. He came with good references, and came to view the property with his mum who also stood as his guarantor. He claimed that he had never rented before, as he had always lived with his family.

He paid his first month's rent in advance, and everything checked out ok. My disapproving ex-colleagues wouldn't tell me what he had been arrested for, so I went back to my office (my dining room table at home) turned to my PC, and simply googled his name. To my horror, I found that he had just served six months of a twelve-month prison sentence for head-butting a fourteen-year-old girl in the face, breaking her nose, and beating up the arresting officer! All of this was on Google!

He had been released on licence after serving half of his sentence, but must have breached his licence terms so, subsequently, had been carted off to serve the rest of his sentence under Her Majesty's pleasure.

This also left me with another dilemma. I now had a room that I couldn't fill. I couldn't end the tenancy simply because he had been taken to jail. I called his mother, who stood as guarantor, who now told me that she couldn't afford to pay his rent as she was a single parent! I explained that she was a single parent last week too when she signed as guarantor.

We agreed that she would go to the prison and request that her son sign a notice to surrender his contract with immediate effect, which he did, and it was witnessed.

Great. I had the room back. I also had authority to clear his room and remove the belongings to his mother's address. I'm not easily shocked, owing to several years in the police, but I was a little surprised when I found butt plugs and vibrators under his bed! Heaven knows what he was getting up to. A lucky escape!

The moral of this story: ALWAYS Google every tenant. You may be surprised what you find. Having this as a harsh lesson, I'm happy to say that over the following years we developed a system that takes out all of the poor tenant prospects before they even manage to get a viewing.

This was the final straw that led me to resign fully from the police. After all, I now had three times my police salary from my rental properties.

**Tenant recruitment and referencing**

We were attracting all of our tenants from one platform www.spareroom.co.uk and we didn't need to look down any other angle as it was working well you can also use other resources.

- www.gumtree.co.uk
- www.upad.co.uk
- Facebook.
- Write to the HR dept. of local blue-chip companies
- Advertise in shops on postcards.
- Current tenants' referrals. We pay £50 for every successful referral made by an existing tenant.
- Local letting agents will also source tenants on your behalf.

When the tenant prospect makes contact with us, regardless of the platform they use, they will want to arrange a viewing. Let me make a suggestion: at this point, you should ask some pre-qualifying questions. Let's not waste our time doing the viewing only to find at the referencing stage that they are not suitable. I have pondered over this for ages now, and it seems that I'm the only person in the world that doesn't want to waste my staff's valuable time turning up to unnecessary viewings!

Here are some top questions to ask your potential tenants BEFORE you agree to the viewing. You can do this over the phone or via email or, if you are really brave, you can use the systems that we have set up which do it automatically for you. Take a look at www.newerapropertysolutions.co.uk for more info on this. You will find that these questions will filter out around 80% of your applicants, but that's ok as it means you will be left with the 20% that will be the best tenants who continue to pay their rent on time each month!

Please remember that you will need to be covered by Data Protection legislation before you begin taking personal details from tenants.

Log onto the Information Commissioner's Office website in order to register: www.ico.org.uk

While we are on the boring legislation, a reminder that you may need to register with a government-approved redress scheme such as www.theprs.co.uk or similar.

**Our pre-qualifying questions**

- Prospect's name?
- Prospect's age?
- Current employment and job title?
- Are you on a probationary period at work?
- What is your yearly income?
- Have you ever paid your rent late?
- Are you currently up to date with your rent?
- Have you ever been asked to leave a property?
- Have you ever been evicted from a property?
- Do you have a criminal record?
- Do you use drugs?
- Are you in receipt of housing benefit?
- Do you require a visa to allow you to reside in the UK?

We will also cover this in-depth later. This list can be added to but seriously, why wouldn't you ask these questions up front?

If they answer yes to any of the questions, then we will need further information before we can go ahead with the viewing.

If you are not happy with the responses, then simply explain that they have failed the pre-qualifying questions and you are not able to offer them a property at this time.

Let's say you are happy with the answers provided, the viewing can now go ahead, and you will arrange to meet the prospect at the property. Always text them two hours before to confirm they are attending. (our system does this automatically). If they don't reply, then please don't waste your time.

You will then meet the prospect at the house; this is a great opportunity to see them face to face and see how they present themselves. You can now ask them any other questions that you may have missed. If they have got this far, then the chances are that they are going to be the kind of tenant that you are looking for. If they want to take the room, you can now give them the application form. We use a link on which we send a text message. They can take the application form away with them but to hold the room, we would normally request this back within thirty-six hours.

If you are using a paper form, they will need to post it or drop it back to you. If you are using our system, then this will come back to you as soon as they click send.

You can now choose to reference the tenant prospect yourself, or you can choose to use a referencing company.

We manage our properties ourselves with the help of some part-time, and some full-time staff, so we do our own in-house referencing.

Make sure that the application form gives their consent for you to conduct the necessary checks.

Here are some of my best tips:

Before you begin to pay for your referencing, always check your tenant prospect on Google first, as it's free and, as per the example I gave you earlier. You may be surprised what you find!

- Always seek references from current employers.
- Always seek references from current landlords.
- Where possible, we like to seek a reference from their previous landlord too; if they are a bad tenant, then their current landlord may be very motivated to get rid of them. Their previous landlord won't be so motivated, so is more likely to tell you warts and all!
- Check the tenant's pay slips and/or bank statements to prove that they can afford the rent and this also helps prove their income.
- Credits score them we use www.lettingref.com. It's about £11 per check and you get all the information you need such as County Court Judgements, bankruptcies and address history.

## Right to Rent Act

In 2016, it became a legal requirement to check everyone's immigration status to ensure that they have the legal right to rent property in the UK.

We have certain responsibilities as landlords that we must comply with. You must check that a tenant or a lodger can legally rent your residential property in England.

Before the start of a new tenancy, you must check all applicants over the age of 18 even if:

- They are not named on the tenancy.
- There is no tenancy agreement or the tenancy agreement isn't in writing.
- You must check every applicant. It is against the law to only check people you think are not UK citizens.
- If the tenant is only allowed to stay in the UK for a limited time, you need to do the check twenty-eight days before the start of the tenancy.
- You don't need to check tenants in social housing or care homes.

We ask to see the applicant's ID at the time of the viewing. This helps to prevent wasting time and saves us turning up to properties if they don't have the required ID. When the tenant arrives at the property, we photograph their ID. This is then uploaded into our right-to-rent form and is date stamped and placed on the tenant's file. If the tenant chooses not to take the room, then the information is deleted.

- Check that the documents you are seeing are genuine and are the original documents.

- Check that they belong to the person applying for the room.
- Check that the document gives the tenant the right to rent. For a definitive list of acceptable documents, please visit the government right-to-rent website.
- Certain countries allow the tenant to reside in England without a permit. Even if the tenant is from any of these permitted countries, you still need to check their ID and record that you have done so.
- You can be fined up to £3,000 for renting to someone not permitted to rent in England.
- If the tenant cannot provide the correct documents, then do not rent to them. Find someone else.
- Make a copy of the documents. You can scan or photograph them.
- For passports, copy every page with the expiry date or applicant's details (e.g. nationality, date of birth and photograph), including endorsements, e.g. a work visa or Certificate of Entitlement to the right of abode in England.
- Copy both sides of biometric residence permits.
- Make a complete copy of all other documents.
- Record the date you made the copy.
- Keep copies of the tenant's documents for the time they are your tenant, and for one year after.
- Depending on which is the longest, you must make a further check just before either the expiry date of your tenant's right to stay in England or twelve months after your previous check. If your tenant has no time restrictions, then you do not have to make any further checks.
- If your tenant does not pass a further check, then you must contact the Home Office.

You can visit the .GOV website or call the Home Office if you have any questions: 0300–069–9799.

You can choose to check the documentation either at the viewing (we do this as our contracts are signed remotely) or you can see it upon check-in; either way, it must be viewed, and recorded, before the granting of the tenancy.

Once you are happy with all the information, you can then arrange to meet the tenant at the house to arrange the check in.

Before the check-in, if you are using paper contracts you will need to populate them and have all the paperwork in order.

**Paperwork and Contracts**

Which contract should you use?

On the 15th January, 1989, the Housing Act was introduced and this meant that all tenancies would now all be "assured tenancies" providing that the tenants met the following criteria:

- They must be an individual.
- The property must be their main or principal residence.
- They must have exclusive possession of at least a part of the property.
- The landlord must not be present.

If the tenant matches this criterion, then the agreement that you should use would be an AST (assured short-hold tenancy). If they don't meet this criterion, then a non-Housing Act agreement should be used.

I have met many landlords and investors that have told me they are using "licences" when they should be using AST contracts, thinking that they will be able to evict the tenant at a moment's notice.

The fact is, it doesn't matter what agreement you use, or even if you actually have one. If the tenant is in occupation and they are paying rent and they meet the above criteria, then the courts will likely deem the contract as an AST, so beware those using licences. If the tenant meets the above criteria, then they will be covered by the Housing Act and therefore their tenancy will be protected for six months regardless of you issuing a licence. If you attempt to evict them without serving the correct Section 21 or Section 8 notice, then this will be unlawful.

For those not yet paperless, and using our recommended systems, I advise populating the contracts and then emailing them well before the check-in date to allow the tenant to read and understand them.

**Check-in day**

Arrange to meet the tenant at the property and remind them to bring their ID for one final check.

There are certain prescribed documents that we are required to give to the tenants when signing the tenancy.

The Deregulation Act of 2015 stipulates that from the 1st October, 2015, all landlords and agents that issue AST contracts must provide the following prescribed information to the Tenant. If you fail to provide this, then you will not be able to evict the tenant under Section 21 of the Housing Act 1988.

- A current Energy Performance Certificate (EPC) (the odd thing is even if you are providing all-inclusive bills, the legislation doesn't discount this).
- Government 'how to rent' booklet.
- Deposit protection information.
- Current gas safety certificate

You can print these documents and hand them to the tenant when they check in, but make sure they sign to say that they have received a copy.

If you take deposits, then you will also need to make sure that you have lodged this with a government-approved scheme and you will need to serve the necessary paperwork to the tenant within the required time frame.

Once you have served all the prescribed information and the tenant has signed to say that they have received it, you must then check the smoke alarms/fire detection system in the presence of the tenant to check they are functioning correctly. You should also show the tenant how to activate and silence it, if required.

If you have fire extinguishers in your property, you should train the tenant how to use them and ask them to sign a document upon doing so.

We then go through the house and check that everything works. It's important to say at this point that as we don't take deposits, there is no need for us to conduct an inventory. I'm not saying that this is right or wrong, but it works well for us.

If you do take deposits, then it's important that you conduct an inventory of the tenant's room and the communal areas and get the tenant to sign and, where possible, have a witness sign too.

At this point, we will set up a standing order with the tenant. You can use direct debit systems, but they will charge you for each transaction. As we have such a large portfolio, we choose to set up standing orders as they are free of charge. We do this upon check-in, and it takes literally three minutes. Once the tenant signs the standing order mandate, we post it to the bank on their behalf. This way, at least we know it's been done.

Make sure the standing order stipulates payment is to be made on the first of each month. This way, you only need to check your bank account and reconcile once, instead of every day!

Finally, we will show the tenant the "house folder". This is where we populate all the necessary documentation for the property. It's a small plastic presentation folder that can be bought from any stationers with see-through plastic envelopes inside. This will allow you to insert certificates, and it consists of the following:

- Manager's contact details and contact numbers
- Maintenance policy and contact numbers
- EPC
- Electrical testing certificate
- Alarm testing certificate
- Emergency lighting testing certificate
- Fire extinguisher testing certificate
- Gas Safe Certificate

- PAT testing certificate
- HMO licence (one should also be displayed in the common area)
- Property Redress Scheme Certificate
- Our Harmonious House rules
- Useful info, such as bin day and location of stop-taps etc.

You then leave them to it! That's it.

We are 99% paperless with our tenant on boarding, as much of the above is done in advance, and I'll explain a little more about this later.

## Managing the house

The first thing we consider with a new HMO is having key safes installed at the front or rear of the property and one for each room inside.

One of our biggest reasons for call-outs are tenants locking themselves out of the property. With the key safes installed, all our maintenance team has to do is provide them with the safe code and they can let themselves back in. Our team will then go to the property the following day and change the code.

Be careful that the tenant doesn't see this as an alternative way of storing their keys, though. I would suggest if there is more than one call-out by the same tenant per month that they are charged for the service. Please check with your insurance provider before installing keys safes.

## Mandatory checks

To comply with legislation, you will be required to conduct periodic checks of the fire safety equipment in your property and keep records.

The following guidelines have been sourced from the **LACORS** recommendations, which is the benchmark used by Local Councils for fire safety.

Always check with your local housing team at your council to determine their policy as they may differ slightly.

**Grade A** alarm system (Panel) one call point or detector in each zone should be tested weekly. The test should be recorded along with any defects in the log book and action taken to rectify the problem.

A six-monthly service should be carried out by a qualified alarm technician in accordance with BS 5839: part 1 this should be recorded in the log book, and a certificate of testing should be issued.

**Grade D** System (Mains interlinked). These systems should be tested every month using the test button on the sensor. All alarms should be cleaned periodically in accordance with the manufacturer's instructions. The test should be recorded along with any defects in the log book and action taken to rectify the problem.

A twelve-monthly service should be carried out by a qualified alarm technician and a certificate of testing should be issued.

## Emergency lights

## Monthly

All emergency lighting systems must be tested monthly. The test is a short functional test in accordance with BS EN 50172:2004 / BS 5266-8:2004.

## Annually

Lights must be tested with a full three-hour battery discharge. The lights should still be functional at the end of this test. These results must be recorded along with any defects in the emergency light log book, along with any defects and how the problem is to be rectified.

We have our lights tested each month by our own engineer and then serviced every six months along with the fire panels.

You will be required to have a copy of the fire alarm and emergency lights log book at the premises for inspection by the tenants.

## Portable Appliance Testing (PAT)

There is no legal requirement to have a house PAT tested as long as a competent person checks all plugs and electrical items prior to a tenant checking in.

However, landlords have a legal requirement to ensure electrical equipment is safe and it has to be assessed. The Health and Safety Exec (HSE) state that a risk-based approached should be used. I do recommend that you have your property PAT tested by a qualified engineer as it's not expensive and is best practice; we like to make sure that our houses are safe. Your local council may require a PAT test before issuing a licence.

## Electrical Testing

The property will need to have a current electrical testing certificate. This usually lasts five years, depending on the date and condition of the installation

## Gas Safety

All gas appliances will need to be serviced and inspected every twelve months by a qualified Gas Safety engineer.

The certificate must be displayed at the property.

## Source LACORS

## Routine maintenance and cleaning

It's a great idea to have a cleaner at least once a fortnight. This way, you will be confident that the house will be maintained to a good standard. It also helps when it comes to marketing and selling rooms.

Make your life easier by asking the cleaner to supply all their own products, including bin bags! Even professional tenants don't buy bin bags, but they will still fill the bin with rubbish! This then causes problems in the house, so for the sake of £3 a roll, add them to the list.

Ask the cleaner to change the bins and tidy the bin area outside.

## Regular house inspections

It is up to you how often you should inspect the house/rooms of your HMO. If you have your cleaner and your maintenance person regularly visiting the property, then you should also use them as your eyes and your ears. If the cleaner spots a maintenance issue, then they should report it to you or your maintenance person.

You don't have to give notice to a tenant in order to check the communal areas of a shared property, but it is polite and courteous to do so. You do need to give at least twenty-four hours' notice to check their own room that is listed on their AST contract – unless in the case of an emergency when access is needed immediately.

If you have professional tenants, then I wouldn't recommend carrying out any more than one room inspection every four to six months, unless you feel it necessary to conduct more as we don't want to be harassing them. It is their home after all.

## Routine maintenance

## (This is ancillary to the routine safety testing.)

We mentioned cleaning earlier; it's a great idea to ask your cleaner to wash up too! (There will always be dishes in the sink.) Ask your maintenance person to conduct regular monthly checks on the following:

- Shower traps are free from hair; this will prevent any blockage.
- Toilets flush freely.
- Sinks drain freely.

- All door handles and locks are checked, including locks on bathroom doors.
- Kitchen cupboard handles are secure.
- Any fire doors wedged open by the tenants are to be closed. Automatic closers visual check, in case they have worked loose.
- Filters on any condensing tumble dryers to be cleaned.
- Taps are secure and tight on all sinks.
- All bulbs to be checked and replaced if necessary.
- Any visual signs of leaking, or stains on ceilings.
- Outside areas are tidy and free from rubbish.

If your property has a garden, then it will need to be maintained. Ask your maintenance person if they will also do this; if not, hire a gardener. Don't let it become overgrown, as this will put prospective tenants off.

Make sure that you have some form of maintenance system and please don't let that be you! If you start answering maintenance calls and going to houses to fix problems, you will only ever be a landlord. You will never be an entrepreneur as all your time will be spent in the business rather than on it.

Here's what we did when we started out.

Remember earlier in the book, during the marketing section, I mentioned using a local trade magazine? In that same magazine, I can guarantee you will find a few people offering property maintenance services.

First, buy a cheap contract phone in your business name. Call and ask the property maintenance person if you can give them the phone. When your tenants check in, they are given the number for all maintenance issues and call maintenance direct to that phone.

Agree an on-call retaining fee and hourly rate with the maintenance person and that's it. You have your maintenance covered!

Why buy a phone instead of using his/hers I hear you ask? Well, if they go sick, or if they go on holiday, you can simply take the phone and give it to someone else for that period of time, without having to tell your tenants anything. It's dead simple and very effective!

# Chapter 12
# Systems

W e touched on the manual check-in procedure earlier. Now I wanted a deeper look to show you exactly how we operate our business.

I remember the day. I was doing everything we teach you not to do! I was at a rent-to-rent property that we had recently acquired. It was half-term, so my kids were in one of the bedrooms and throwing KFC wings at each other. My dog, Molly, was downstairs continually barking at the next door neighbour's cat that was intent on a staring competition. I was in the upstairs bedroom with a cheese sandwich in one hand and a paintbrush in the other. (This is not how it should be done). I had high hopes for this house as it had six bedrooms, four of which were en-suite, and it was in the city centre, so demand should be really high.

Based on this assumption, I advertised the rooms on www.spareroom.co.uk, even though they were not going to be ready for another four to six weeks. I was transparent in the advert and explained that we were taking early reservations for the house.

Sure enough, the phone didn't stop ringing, and I was faced with a dilemma. I had no system in place, as such – it really was just me and my phone which kept ringing. Sometimes I was just too busy to answer and let it go to voicemail. The problem with this was that I either called the prospect back too late and they had already found alternative accommodation, or I didn't get around to calling them back at all. Sound familiar?

It dawned on me that I was potentially losing loads of prospects, and I decided I needed to create some form of system.

Over the following few weeks, I did manage to fill the house in one day. I did a block viewing on a Saturday morning where seven people turned up. Out of the seven, five people took the rooms, four of whom are still with me to this day. Hosting a block viewing creates a little bit of competition and scarcity which worked really well for us.

Over the next six months, I worked into the early hours of the morning scouring the internet for a suitable tenant-on-boarding system. Something that would create automatic bookings into my online calendar and something that allowed me to send tenant applications directly via an online web-based form. I wanted to be able to conduct the due diligence on each tenant BEFORE any viewing; this is where most people get it wrong. What is the point in wasting all that time doing viewings and completing forms only to find the prospect would never be suited anyway? I wanted to plug this gap, but I found nothing. Just the usual property management systems that weren't geared up for this sort of task.

I decided to create my own, but using third-party platforms. Bearing in mind, I am no developer when it comes to computers, this was a laborious task for me that evolved over the following eighteen months. I managed to create a system using several different platforms that went on to change the way we ran and operated our ever-growing portfolio.

Here's how it works:

1. The tenant prospect contacts us through or our website, or www.spareroom.co.uk, and shows their interest.

2. We reply with this message "Hi, thank you for showing an interest in our property; we would love you to come and have a look at the room.

   To make it easy, you can click the below link and choose a day and time that suits you.
   We look forward to seeing you soon.
   Kind regards
   Rick and Lorraine."

3. We include the link to our booking page at the bottom of the message.

4. The prospect will then click on the link and is taken to our online booking site which lists all the available rooms we have, along with selected time slots that they can choose. The time slots are not random; they link to our office diary. If we already have appointments for their chosen time, then the system will not allow us to double book; it will only show free time that we have available in the diary.

5. When the prospect books a slot, they will be invited to answer around seventeen "pre-qualifying online questions". I share those questions here for you:

   • What is your name?
   • What is your mobile telephone number?

- What is your email address?
- Please give details of your current employment including job title.
- Please give details of your current status, e.g. are you a homeowner or a tenant?
- When do you need to move?
- Have you ever missed a rent payment or fallen behind with your rent?
- Why do you need to move?
- Do you have a criminal record?
- Do you have any bad debt or County Court Judgements?
- The rent is paid monthly in advance; do you have sufficient funds?
- Do you have a suitable guarantor?
- We will need to check your "Right to Rent Status." Please confirm your nationality here.
- Do you require a visa to reside in the UK?
- If so, please state the expiry date of your visa here.
- How many hours a week do you work?
- Are you in receipt of any form of housing benefit or income support?

As you can see, we are asking a lot of questions before we agree to the viewing. This saves us so much wasted time with applicants that just wouldn't be suited to the property.

We find that by asking these questions upfront, it eliminates about 80% of applications; the 20% left are the market that suits us.

The remaining prospects that do go on to complete the form always make for excellent tenants. We have not had any arrears, in the whole of our portfolio for over three years! Some of this will be down to our proactive management, but a lot is due to the pre-qualifying systems that we use every day.

Not everyone will be truthful, but they will be discovered further along the due diligence journey!

1. As soon as the prospect completes the online questions and hits the submit button, they will be sent an automated text message. This will have the date, time and address of the viewing. The lettings manager (you) will also receive an automated text telling you that someone has booked a viewing. They are also requested to bring their passport and/or visa with them to prove their right to rent status should they want to proceed with the room.

2. This appointment will now be automatically populated into the office diary with a copy of all the questions and answers so that you or your staff can read them and decide if the viewing is to go ahead or not.

3. If you decide that the prospect is not suitable, then you simply go onto the system and cancel the viewing. The prospect will receive a text explaining that they have failed the vetting procedure (they can't reply to that text).

4. If you decide that they look like a good prospect, then you do nothing.

5. Two hours before the viewing the prospect will receive an automated text message reminding them that they have a viewing. They are instructed to reply to the text message with the words "CONFIRM". If they don't follow this action then the viewing is cancelled; this saves an enormous amount of time in wasted

viewings. When they reply, the lettings manager (you) will receive the reply "CONFIRM" and you know everything is good to go.

6. You or your staff will meet the prospect at the designated time at the property and conduct the viewing.

7. The prospect decides that they like the room and they would like to go ahead and reserve it.

8. You send them a link via a text message to the "Reservation Form", which they can complete on their phone/tablet. The form is just their name, contact details and the room details and address of the house they want to reserve. They are invited, by the form, to upload a copy of their visa/passport or other suitable documentation required by the Right to Rent Act. The form allows them to use the camera facility on their phone to take a photo of the ID, this is then uploaded into the form and keeps all the information together. And as you are there, you have confirmed the ID is sufficient and confirmed it is the same person. There is a reason we do this at the viewing stage.

The Right to Rent Act states that we must physically see the ID in person (or electronically over a live feed) before we grant the tenancy.

As we complete, and grant, our contracts online with electronic signature we won't be seeing the tenant again until the day they check in.

9. As soon as the tenant completes the reservation form, they will then receive an automatic email with a link to the full application form, which we ask them to complete within 72 hours. We now remove the room

from our marketing page. And we will now manually Google the tenant prospect (remember my earlier story!) This is very, very important! Google may tell you if the tenant has been in trouble in the past with the police!

The application form is, once again, completed online, and we ask the normal questions. As soon as the tenant completes the details for their current employer that person will receive an automatic email with a link for a reference request. As soon as the tenant completes the details for their current landlord, that person will receive an email with a link for a reference request. The whole process is automated!
The form requests that the tenant upload their current pay slips and any other supporting documentation that will assist in their application.

At this point, I add that all the forms are heavily encrypted to protect the tenant's details.

10. As soon as the tenant completes the form, you will receive an email that will alert you.
11. At this point, we need to transcribe the information from the application form to the AST contract.
12. The AST contract is uploaded into the signing platform along with the following documents:

- New Tenant Welcome Letter
- House Policy
- Maintenance Policy
- E.P.C (Energy Performance)
- Government How to Rent handbook

- Gas safety certificate
- Electric safety certificate
- Fire Alarm Testing Certificate
- Emergency Lights testing certificate
- PAT testing certificate (Portable appliance)
- HMO Licence
- Security policy
- Manager's Contact details

13. When they receive the email, they simply open the platform and sign the contracts and sign to say they have received all the documentation.

14. The platform records the time, date, and IP address of the person when they:

    1. Receive the email
    2. Open it
    3. Sign it

    This form of electronic signature is now fundamentally accepted for this type of contract. Please consult a legal advisor if you have any doubts.

15. All the necessary paperwork has now been completed, and we arrange to meet the tenant at their new home. Prior to the meeting, we send the tenant our bank details and request that the first month's rent is transferred before we meet.

16. Upon arrival, we will show the tenant around the property and we will complete an electronic "Check-in form". The form will ask the following questions with a drop down bar allowing the tenant to answer Y/N.

- Property address
- Tenant name
- Room number
- Date
- Is the property fitted with a fire detection device? Y/N
- Has the device been tested in your presence? Y/N
- Is the device working correctly? Y/N
- Have you been shown how to activate or silence the device if required to do so? Y/N
- Non-smoking policy
- Keys and security policy (Stating that they must keep the external doors locked)
- Saniflow toilet (Electric toilet) policy stating that only natural waste may be flushed
- Fire extinguisher policy (explained below)

You will notice that we have no provision for an inventory here. The form will lend itself nicely if you want to add an inventory to it or you can, of course, outsource the inventory to a professional company.

We choose not to take a deposit for the whole of our portfolio. That's not to say that's the right thing to do, but it certainly works for us. As we don't take deposits, it means we are more attractive to tenants and we don't have any redress so it would simply be a waste of our time to conduct an inventory!

You must choose what's best for you and your business. If you choose to take a deposit, you must lodge this with one of the government-approved deposit schemes within the correct time limit. You must always ensure that you have served the prescribed information regarding the deposit to the tenant also within the correct time limit. Failure to do this correctly may result in you not being able to evict the tenant in the future under section 21.

**Fire extinguisher policy**

Our council stipulates that we have to provide fire extinguishers. Some councils don't like the idea of tenants fighting a fire and have instructed landlords to remove them. As we have to provide them, we also have to provide tenants with training on how to use them! This has been itemised in all of our fire risk assessments.

The process is relatively easy. When we check the tenant in, we give them the necessary instructions on how to use the extinguishers, and they sign the check-in form to confirm that they have had the training.

We also stipulate that the extinguishers are simply to aid their exit from the property and not to fight a fire.

1. We now fill in the only piece of physical paper that we have and that's the standing order form. Unfortunately, the bank requires this to be a wet signature, as I mentioned earlier.

   Why a standing order? Direct debit companies charge per transaction and rightfully so after all they are a business. Standing orders are free.

   We have always used standing orders and we have never had a problem and we save hundreds of pounds a month by not using direct debits.

We always charge rents from the first of every month, and I suggest that you do the same. This way you only have to reconcile your accounts once a month, rather than every day. If the tenant moves in halfway through the month, then simply charge them for the remaining days up until the first of the following month.

You will thank me for this in years to come.

That's it! Don't forget to post the standing order form. That's the system that I created. You will see that it is a replication of the manual system, but online instead of using paper. This saves us so much time.

If you would like more information on how you can adopt these systems for yourself, then please visit my website www.newerapropertysolutions.co.uk

The tenant is now safely checked in. We download all the completed forms and create a nice tenant folder in Dropbox. This is another great tool, as it allows you to send a link via a text message to the tenant which contains their contract if they ever ask for a copy. We are 99.99% paperless; I'm just waiting for the bank to accept an electronic signature for standing orders.

Also a note here: if you choose to take a guarantor then this should be on a separate guarantor deed which will need to be signed and witnessed, as this is a deed it will also need to be a 'wet' signature.

## What happens if my tenant doesn't pay?

If you use the systems I described earlier, then you will reduce your exposure to bad tenants, but sometimes shit happens! And we have to deal with it when it arises. Tenants are humans like everyone else and sometimes their circumstances change.

We must remain professional and always act within the law. If your tenant misses a payment, the first thing you must do is contact them. Someone from the office will call and remind them that their rent hasn't been paid.

It's important not to jump at them straight away, as sometimes people do make mistakes, including banks! So usually, on the second of the month, if a payment still hasn't arrived, it would just mean a friendly call or even a text as a reminder. Usually, this does the trick and the payment arrives not long afterwards.

If that's not the case, then a second follow-up call a couple of days later would take place. If it's an oversight on the tenant's behalf, then we can agree to take payment over the phone and everything goes back to normal.

If for any reason the tenant can't pay, owing to unforeseen circumstances, maybe a job change or similar, then we can in certain cases agree to a structured repayment plan.

Those are the easier ones to deal with. If the tenant chooses not to keep the dialogue open and ignores your calls, then the next step would be a letter explaining that their account is now in arrears and it needs to be brought up to date.

If that is ignored and if you have taken a guarantor, you should now be contacting the guarantor to explain the situation and be looking at them for payment. Hopefully, the guarantor will get things sorted and you will receive the money. I would be cautious here though. The guarantor may have paid but will this mean the tenant will pay next month? You will have to monitor the situation closely.

If they have decided not to pay and you cannot agree to any repayment terms, then it's time to consider eviction.

My advice, if you are at this stage and relatively new to managing tenants, hire a professional eviction company on your behalf to help you through the process. If you get the paperwork wrong, then it can be a very frustrating process for you and it may mean you have to start all over again. It's worth a small fee to pay the professionals to do this for you' take a look on the internet for recommendations.

This is where it's important to have served all the necessary paperwork to the tenant when they check in as listed earlier.

## Section 21 eviction

You can evict tenants that have an AST (Assured Shorthold Tenancy) using a section 21 Notice if you want the property back after the fixed term ends, and after their statutory six-month period is over. Note that the tenant will need to be in a "periodic" agreement (month by month) with no fixed end date.

If the tenancy started after April 2007, and if you take deposits, you can only use a Section 21 notice if you put the tenant's deposit in a deposit protection scheme.

## Serving a Section 21 notice

A Section 21 notice must give your tenants at least two months' notice to leave your property. You must explain that you're giving notice under Section 21 of the Housing Act 1988.

A section 21 notice can't be served until month four of the tenancy with the prescribed two-month notice period. This will take the tenant to month six, which is their statutory period. A Section 21 is a "no-fault" notice which means that you don't need a reason, you simply just want your property back. If the tenant doesn't leave at the end of the S21 notice period, then you will have to apply to the courts for an eviction order.

## Section 8 eviction

If your tenants have broken the terms of their tenancy, there are prescribed grounds for possession under section 8. You must make sure that you use the correct grounds before applying for a section 8 eviction. Please take a look at www.gov/evicting tenants for grounds under section 8 and familiarise yourself with the process. Section 8 can be served during the statutory six-month period, providing the necessary grounds exist.

Ensure that when serving notice, it is done via recorded delivery post and allow two days on the notice period for the letter to reach the tenant.

The above eviction procedures can be complicated, and it's important that they are executed correctly. I have deliberately not gone into more detail here as I firmly believe that as a new investor, you should always seek the assistance from an eviction expert or online eviction platform. Mistakes can be costly and may result in prolonging the process, which in turn will cause more void periods, loss of money, and stress to yourself!

Always follow the letter of the law and don't harass your tenant as this could come back to cause you problems.

## Should you pursue a tenant that has left owing you money?

The simple answer is…maybe. I know this is non-committal, but it does depend on the circumstances. If the tenant has left owing a considerable amount of money, then my answer would be 'yes, absolutely' as this sends out a message to others that may think this behaviour is acceptable.

If the amount owed is not too significant, then my advice would be to let it go and concentrate your energy on filling rooms with a better type of tenant next time.

If it is a significant amount (that would be highly subjective), then I would be tempted to enter into a Money Claim Online case.

(MCOL) this is a very simple procedure, but it won't guarantee that you will be compensated as there are many variables.

The process is easy and it's all conducted online.

You cannot use MCOL if the tenant is:

- Under the age of 18
- Eligible for legal aid
- Making a claim for injury or accident

You also cannot claim against anyone under the age of 18 or from anyone who lacks 'mental capacity.'

The steps are easy to register a claim. First, you will be required to register yourself, then you will be asked for the defendant's (tenant's) details and their current, or last, known address. You will then be required to complete the "claim particulars". Here, you will list what money is owed to you and why; it is likely at this point that you will be required to provide a statement called "The Particulars of Claim". This will include the amount you are claiming. You are also asked if you will be claiming interest; don't forget to add the registration fee to the amount owed as the tenant should also be paying this.

Once you have completed these questions, you will be invited to pay the fee for your application. The amount will depend on the claim.

Once registered, the court will send a claim pack to the defendant (tenant) at their last known address.

The defendant then has fourteen days from the date of service to file a response. The defendant can extend the time to respond to twenty-eight days by filing an acknowledgement of service. If this happens, you will be notified.

The defendant is then required to submit a written response to your claim. They can also file this online.

If they file a dispute to your claim, then you may agree to a court hearing, but first, it's likely that you will be offered to go to "mediation" to see if this dispute can be settled amicably out of court. The mediation is usually over the phone with a court representative, you, and the defendant. The representative will call either you or the defendant first individually. They will ask if you are prepared to accept an offer, then they will call the defendant and so the negotiating process goes on until you reach an agreement. The mediator will then complete the paperwork, organise the payment and hopefully it will land into your account not long afterwards. If the payment doesn't land into your account, then the defendant will automatically be issued with a CCJ. You can then apply for a warrant to send the enforcement officers (bailiffs) around to seize goods to the value of the debt.

If the defendant doesn't respond within the fourteen-day period, then a judgement can be awarded against them. If the defendant refuses to mediate and refuses to accept responsibility, then you may have to attend court and let the judge decide.

The amount of energy you put into this can sometimes be draining, so while I'm an advocate of pursuing every penny, you will need to ask yourself when is the time to walk away and maybe just let it go. That's up to you!

So that's the money and eviction side of things covered. Also, remember that if you agree to a tenant leaving while in their fixed term, you should always ask them to sign a document stating that they are voluntarily surrendering their tenancy.

This is just in case they ever come back and try to claim that you have evicted them unlawfully.

Regardless of which path you take, remember that we are professionals and you must always act with integrity and within the letter of the law. If you are still not sure of your rights, then contact a solicitor.

## Keeping a harmonious house and dealing with disputes

Shared houses are not all wine and roses,! Nor will they make you a millionaire overnight. They can be a fruitful source of income if they are managed correctly, but they are more work than your standard single let.

Here are some examples of complaints that we have received from tenants over the years:

- "Someone keeps eating my cheese."
- "The guy downstairs is making funny noises in his sleep and you need to sort it out."
- "Someone stole my cucumber that I was growing in the vegetable garden outside."
- "My clothes are stuck in the washing machine and they are all designer. They will now be ruined, so I want to know how you will be compensating me."
- "I lost my keys last night, so I couldn't get in, but when I eventually did, I noticed that the back kitchen door had been kicked in. I think someone tried to burgle us, but nothing has been taken."
- "I can't live in this mess. Someone has left a pea on the stove, what sort of house is this?" (He actually sent a photo of one pea on the hob).

- "When is the cleaner due? I think she is due today. This is urgent because we have no bin bags.?
- "I don't know what's going on, but every morning when I wake up my pillow is wet."
- "The guy upstairs keeps getting drunk and when he does he snores like a train; please can you sort this out!"
- "Please, can you ask the boys to lift up the toilet seat when they use the bathroom?"
- "The lock on the front door is broken, and I'm late for work." The reply to this was, "Use the back door," to which the tenant replied: "There is a back door?"
- "The guy downstairs plays video games until 3 am. and I can't get to sleep with the constant pew, pew, pew, pew, noise coming from his room!"

I could go on and on, but that's a small example of the daily messages we get from tenants. I guess it would be a dull life without them.

How do we manage this without becoming Mum and Dad? We can't act on every complaint, but we always respond with a polite and courteous message and if required we will send a letter to the tenants reminding them of the responsibilities they have while living in our house.

Normally this is enough to appease the person reporting and they just want to get it off their chest. Most of the messages are sent in the heat of the moment when tensions are running high.

You will remember earlier in the book that I mentioned a house policy. This is a document explaining our house rules and how to be courteous with the other housemates. We can refer to specific paragraphs in the document if we need to be a little more direct.

Usually, a polite reminder is all it takes and the status quo is restored.

If you have a particularly unruly housemate that regularly is the butt of complaints, then you may have to take a more proactive approach. You have to tread carefully here as there are always two sides to every story and it would be unprofessional of you to take sides. This could come back to bite you and the tenant could accuse you of harassment.

However, sometimes you may need to be proactive, and if the evidence is clear that one housemate is upsetting everyone else, you need to deal with it quickly, as the others may just up and leave. If you have exhausted all options, then this may mean you have to consider eviction, providing it is lawful.

I do know lots of investors and private landlords that will hold a "house meeting" when things start to go wrong. I would tread carefully with this as you do it once, every time something goes wrong, they will be on the phone expecting you to do it again. I have never conducted such meetings and explain to the tenants that we can neither be their mum or their dad and we always suggest they try to mediate it themselves first. In my experience, as soon as you delegate the responsibility back to them, they generally quieten down. Start as you mean to go on.

## Keeping it real

I firmly believe that with anything in life, you should be given the whole picture. It's my duty not just to show and case study the good stuff with House Shares and HMOs, but also to share the bad stuff and when things go wrong they can go very wrong!

HMOs can be a great way to eventually replace your income, but this is not, I repeat NOT, going to make you a gazillionaire overnight. Far from it!

HMOs require a sound knowledge of the Housing Act, the Housing standards, the Lacors Fire Safety recommendations, article 4 planning direction, Mandatory Licensing, additional and selective licensing, local policy, HHSRS etc. Most of which are listed in this book, but this book is only a guide. It's up to you to continue your knowledge and to become a competent and ethical landlord/investor.

Tenants come in all sorts of shapes and sizes, some are good others not so good, but it will be your responsibility to look after them come thick or thin. Becoming a landlord, or a property investor, carries enormous responsibility.

Always have a cash buffer. You will need it when that boiler breaks down in the middle of the coldest winter on record and you have six tenants in the house with no heating and no water. These repairs must be made, and emergency repairs such as this come at a cost.

HMOs will never be a 100% passive income; anyone that tells you so are liars. You can, of course, leverage much of your time to a property manager or an agent, but ultimately you own the property and the buck will stop with you.

In my experience, most tenants just want a quiet life. They want and, rightfully expect, good standards of safe, lawful, and clean accommodation. If you provide this and go about your investing in the correct way, then you should reap the rewards over time.

## Mindset

"If you think you can or if you think you can't, you are right" – Henry Ford.

When you begin your investing, you will experience many emotions and many self-limiting beliefs. You will begin with lots and lots of energy and enthusiasm. This will turn into moments of anxiety and despair as you move through your journey.

You may be blessed with a supportive partner, or you may not.

Property investing can be lonely, but like anything in life, you must persist and remain focused. Switch your mind off from negativity.

You will be faced with many challenges along your way. Some will turn into great ventures, others not so. Education is the key. This book has given you some insights into setting up your portfolio of HMOs, but it is by no means exhaustive. Explore the opportunities that are out there regarding further education.

Please take a look at www.newerapropertysolutions.co.uk or contact me for information on our classroom-based education and mentoring programmes.

If you get knocked down, then dust yourself off and get back on the horse. You only ever fail if you give up.

If you would like to see how I can help you along your journey, then please feel free to contact me. I always have an open door. I have a structured HMO Mentoring programme that will guide you along the way and help you build a sustainable and profitable HMO portfolio with me to hold your hand along the way. For more information please see the contact details at the end of the book.

You never know where your journey will take you. Most of this book was written while I was in Thailand after being commissioned and paid to fly over and teach a high net worth group of English individuals the HMO Strategy! Since my old life as a copper ended, and my new one began, we now have several millions of pounds worth of property and hundreds of happy tenants. I have a life that I could only have dreamed of before. I spend much of my spare time managing and running our newly-founded powerchair football club for disabled children. After all, it was the conversation I had with Ben about football that started this ball rolling!

I need to add at this point that I'm by no means a professional author (I can tell, I hear you cry). I am an ex-police officer that had a vision to change my life for the better. I hope you liked this book. If you did, then please leave a review on Amazon. That way we can help even more people change their life for the better.

Thanks for reading. My contact details are below.

Stay motivated!

Rick.

# CONTACT DETAILS

If you would like to contact me to discuss anything (property related), then please feel free to drop me a line or tag me in a post:-

www.newerapropertysolutions.co.uk (main website)

The HMO Community Group (our Facebook HMO page)

Rick Gannon UK (my public Facebook page)

Rick@newerapropertysolutions.co.uk (my email)

34444032R00097

Printed in Great Britain
by Amazon